To Kim and Mark A.J.
this

With all good wishes

[illegible]

Moving Forward From Behind

Moving Forward From Behind:

Life and Times of African-Americans In Bryan, Texas From 1885 to 1971

by
Oswell Person

OCES Publishers, Inc.

Fort Worth, Texas 76112

Published in the United States by OCES Publishers, Inc.

Printed in the United States of America.

For information contact:

OCES Publishers, Inc.
5901 Riverbend Parkway
Fort Worth, Texas 76112-1053.
operson5901@yahoo.com

Designed by Rebekah Petty
Photos provided by author

Library Congress Cataloging-in-Publication Data

Person, Oswell
Moving Forward From Behind:
Life and Times of African-Americans in Bryan, Texas
From 1885 to1971

Includes bibliographical references and index.

ISBN-978-0-615-37417-8

1. African-American History, 2. Brazos County Texas, 3.Bryan, Texas,
4. Segregated Schools, 5. African-American Teachers,
6. African-American Schools

Also by Oswell Person:
A Brief Analysis of The Historical Development of Higher Education For African-Americans (with William Allan Kritsonis)

Dedication

To Dr. Constance Person (Connie), my wife; Vivian Peterson, my mother; and my principal at Washington Elementary School, Mr. Oliver Wayne Sadberry, who made lasting impressions and incredible differences in my life, with thanks and loving memory.

First, to Connie without whose love success would not have been possible, who demonstrated support by leaving her job, house and moving, with a new born son, to married student housing at Michigan State University. After re-establishing her career in Michigan, moved to California so I could advance my professional career, then to North Carolina. Relocated yet again back to Michigan, and back to Michigan and back to Texas, in each move selling the house and buying a new house in the state/city in which we moved and trying to re-establish professional connections and friendships. Second, to my mother whose faith helped me to be strong and who taught lessons to live by.

To Mr. Oliver W. Sadberry who never gave up on me, and in fact invited me to come back and teach at Washington Elementary School in 1969. Unfortunately, I could not accept his invitation as graduate school was in my immediate future.

Foreword

The idea for this project began in 2008 at the E.A. Kemp High School Business meeting of the Reunion Classes of 1948-49 and the Decade of the Fifties. One of the agenda topics was "Planning" for the 2010 Bryan School for Colored and E.A. KempHigh all school reunion that occurs every five years; the last reunion was in 2005. My original thoughts were to prepare a written record about African-American Life in Bryan from 1930-1971, about four decades, before the next all school reunion in 2010. The idea started to take shape after leaving the 2008 meeting as I attempted to develop an approach that would interlace historical facts from1930-1971 with recollections, oral history, and reflections. It soon became clear that in order to understand conditions that set the stage for African-American life and times in Bryan, and moving forward from behind, it would be necessary to start much sooner than 1930. Hence, starting in1885 when the first Public School for Colored was built and ending in 1971 with the desegregation of schools, provided an authentic point of departure. (Farris 2001-2009, n.p.) In doing so I realized some events, people and places may not get included in one volume. With this in mind, I began this effort knowing I owe an apology to many African-American parents, students, teachers and other citizens who deserved to be included. It is certainly not my intent to offend anyone who bore the same experiences while trying to move forward from behind. Inevitably some one will be left out of the period of time covered, based in part, on recollections and reflections. But, because so many individuals contributed in a variety of ways to helping African-Americans survive this long period of humiliations, insults and harsh disregard for humanity, every effort was made to be inclusive. Events, people and places that are not covered in this edition will be the primary focus of an addendum.

Oftentimes we forget specific events, people, and places that helped shape who we have become. Perhaps in reading the following accounts, you will find considerable delight as you recall significant events and people. Before undertaking this project I, we, thought separation of schools and all things social were not to be questioned. After all that was our total experience at that time. This project allowed me to remember the bad, good, and ugly commonly shared and to review the earlier years in Bryan with different lenses. One of the lenses helped me understand (perhaps what many of us did not) that our parents were examples of the resiliency embodied in an oppressed people. What they endured gave their children and neighbors the strength to overcome obstacles set forth in the 1896 Plessy v. Ferguson "separate but equal doctrine." (Williams 1966, p.715).

In searching recorded information to validate or invalidate my recollections, I found conflicting information in reference to dates and to identification of individuals. For example, in one source the year 1880 is the date when twenty colored students were enrolled in public school (Brazos County Historical Time Line 1880, p.3); in another source 1885 is the date when Bryan Public School for Colored was founded.(Farris 2001-2009, n.p.) Also, the address given for Bryan Public School for Colored is E.19th Street but the school was located between E.19th and 20th Streets on the corner of Houston Street; the main entrance was on Houston Street with two exits. Another example is September, 1971, the date given when Washington Elementary School was destroyed by fire. (Black Education in Bryan 1975). But according to Mr. Sadberry's daughter, the School was destroyed before his death on December 4, 1970. When my classmates and I began first grade at Washington Elementary School there were four secondary frame buildings located on E.19th Street. But the brick building that replaced the 1914 frame building (Bryan Public School for Colored) was between E.19th and 20th Streets, as stated above. (Brundige1986, p.109) The address given for E.A. Kemp Junior-Senior High School is W.19th Street. (Farris September 30, 2009) The school was actually located between W. 20th and 21st Streets bordered by N. Congress Street, which was one of three entrances. Wendell Davis is included as one of the star players in the 1952-53 picture of E.A. Kemp Football team, but Wendell graduated in 1948. (Buford n.d.) According to the same source a 1966 track team picture has Merion Ellis with the name Lawrence Ellis as one of the stars, but Lawrence graduated in 1957. (Buford n.d.) I tried to change (correct) many of the inaccuracies by checking written records, official websites, and through oral history.

Historical facts, recollections, and reflections of African-American life in Bryan, Texas are presented in the following sections: Honor and Recognition, Background and History, Bryan Public School for Colored, First Grade and Washington Elementary School, George Washington Carver Elementary School, Principal Oliver Wayne Sadberry. E. A. Kemp High Junior-Senior

High School, E.A. Kemp Senior High School, R.C. Neal Junior High School, E.A. Kemp Extra-Curricular-Activities, E.A. Kemp High Alumni: Academic and Professional Achievement, Employment Opportunities: Private and Public, African-American Veterans, Small Business Owners: African-Americans and Italian-Americans, Shot "Gun" Rental Houses" and Government Projects, Hospitals and Medical Care, Recreational Activities-Facilities, Newspapers and Information Sources, City Transportation, Elected Officials, National Association for the Advancement of Colored People (NAACP), Negro Chamber of Commerce, Principals, Teachers and Staff, Dry Toilets, Street Lights, Kerosene Lamps, Ice Boxes, Unpaved Streets, Ironies, Contradictions, Paradoxes, Teachers, Parents, Churches and What I Have Learned, Brazos County and Bryan, Texas Populations 1900-2000 and 2005, Surprise Findings, African-Americans Still Rising, Small Businesses and Other Ventures, Public Schools, Government, Higher Education and Private Sector, Conclusion: Thoughts and Afterthoughts. It is my hope that readers living now, who still remember some parts of the time periods covered, will travel memory lane through each section with me; as a result, gain a new awareness and appreciation of times past, although not ever entirely forgetting the experiences in Bryan, Texas. Furthermore, I hope old wounds of invidious treatment, unequal opportunities, and impoverished living conditions have faded deeply into the background of our collective memories.

Acknowledgments

A project of this scope could not have had a positive outcome without the help of many other people. Hence, it is with sincere gratitude and appreciation to the numerous individuals without whose assistance, this effort would have stalled. First, to my immediate family: Connie, my wife, my sons; Erick C. Person, Stephen D. Person who always supported me. A special thanks to Stephen for lending his computer skills to this project.

To my siblings, Betty, Wanda, Pattie Peterson, and Waymon who had the same early experiences in Bryan, Texas. Also to Waymon T. Peterson, who was an outstanding quarterback; served in Vietnam; provided names of other Vietnam Veterans, and members of his football team.

To my brother-in-law, Maurice Green, Sr. who retired as a Supervisor after forty-five years in the Bryan Sanitation Department. With his long history and invaluable memory of city employees he provided the first and last names of staff and their assigned departments. In addition, he was able to provide the full names of many WW-II Veterans for whom I had only the first and or last names. To Wanda for providing the names of her classmates who graduated from college and are teachers. Both Maurice and Wanda made contributions that were incredibly significant and appreciated.

To my first grade classmates: Leroy Sterling who shared books from his personal library, researched materials in the Brazos Valley African Museum and mailed to me. He also helped me to remember businesses, events and people on the Westside. Thanks to Dr. Halcyon Sadberry Watkins for information on the Bessie Matthews and the date of her father's death (December 4, 1970)-my elementary school principal, mentor and friend. To Sarah Greer Graham for remembering the Italian-American who owned the grocery store in her neighborhood. To Faye Thelma Patterson Sabbs for providing names of Elijah Alonzo (E.A.) Kemp Junior-Senior High School College graduates from the classes of 1956, 1957, and 1958. To George Bell who took messages and helped me to remember all the names of the E.A. Kemp " Gang" including himself, brothers John, Sam and William (Will) Dunn, " Gabbey " Kearney, James C. and Jon Mosley, R. (Reval) Newton, brothers Jimmy, Nelson and Pinkney Parnell, who without fail, attended the Friday mid-night movies at the segregated Palace Theater and sat in balcony seats.

To Barbara Wilson Wright for confirming names of Waco Street neighbors and the date Ollie Carter served in the military.

A special thanks to Mrs. Jessie Mae Walton for providing names of Dr. William A. Hammond, Sr.'s children and their professions; reminding me her brother-in-law owned the grocery store on Waco Street and reviewing the names of principals and teachers from 1885-1971. She made sure I knew the first names of the following Washington Elementary School teachers: Mrs. Carter, Mrs. Cass and Mrs. Hall. She also introduced me to her classmate Berthenia Ellis Wallace who contributed useful information.

To James T. Murphy for confirming the name of the boy's club founded by Mr. Oscar Pierce and the name of the Italian-American who owned the grocery store on the corner of E.19th and N. Polk Streets. Also for confirming that Tommie M. Murphy has a master's degree, Vivian Murphy has a BSN, and that he is the first African-American to serve on the Victoria ISD Board.

Thanks to John Jerome Knox for remembering that Lula, was the first name of Mrs. Callier, my seventh grade teacher.

To Rastine Calhoun, Iona Potts, Geraldine Adams and Tommy Traylor who helped confirm and or remember names of football players and girls on the basketball teams.

To Ruby Ellis for sharing phone numbers of her classmates who could verify information sources. Thanks to Rozell Quarles who provided the names of cheerleaders, drill team members, and majorettes from the classes of 1955, 56 and 57.

To James Knox who reminded me that "Knox's Place" the most popular socializing (safe) recreational place for years, was converted to a rooming house.

To Velma Polk Allen who faxed information on E.A. Kemp college graduates.

To Mildred Ross Phillips and Isaiah who shared website information and copy of the Introductory Issue of John M. Moore Out-Look, Volume One, 1946 and her prepared reunion document. She also confirmed the name of the African-American grocery store owner on 28th Street.

To Bobby Joe and Effie Perry for inviting us into their home and providing names of college graduates. They provided names of teachers who taught at R.C. Neal Junior High School and Carver Elementary School. Thanks also for names of athletic coaches; the years E.A. Kemp High won district championships, and sharing their alumni directory.

To William G. Hall who verified names of teachers and informed me he was an assistant principal at George Washington Elementary School, and confirming the first name of Mr. Walter Carr.

To members of the classes of 1945, 1947-48: Clifton Greer, James Greer, Edward L. Colquitt, Rosie Greer and Marion "Buck" Williams for helping to confirm names of their classmates.

To Adolph Johnson, Jr. for confirming the names of his elementary, junior, senior high school teachers, classmates who graduated from college, phone numbers of Linda Asberry, Robert Person and Maurice Green, Jr. and Jo Ann Jordan who could verify information sources and allow use of his yearbook.

To Ocie Hall, Jr. for information about his uncle's café and father's employment at the Bryan Air Force Base.

To Irma Rooks Kearney who supplied names of Westside Veterans and small business owners and a picture of the Galilee Church A Cappella Choir.

Thanks to Bill Page, Texas A and M University staff, for providing valuable references and special assistance.

To Anne Boykin, City of College Station staff, for information about her mother's research about Italian-Americans.

Thanks to Nancy Ross and Shirley Ferguson staff at the Carnegie Center of Brazos Valley History for pertinent references and special assistance.

Thanks to Wayne Sadberry, Curator and Velma Neblett Wilson staff at the Brazos Valley African-American Museum for information sources and assistance.

To Martha Mosley Delley for Carolyn Hammond Montier's phone number from whom vital family information was obtained. Thanks to Dr. Carolyn H. Montier for verifying her father William H. Hammond, Sr. was President of the African-American Medical Association of Texas.

To citizens who read the Billboard entering the city on Highway 6 motto "Bryan-The City With A Future" and pondered as I, "for whom"?

Thanks to Becky Aldrige and Cynthia Bowman, in the Office of Bryan City Secretary, for Amendments 82 and 87.

Thanks to Dr. Violet O'Valle, Ph.D. from Texas A and M University, English Department Chair, Dean Tarrant County College and friend for advice, proof reading and technical assistance.

Thanks to George Vaults for pictures of former E.A. Kemp basketball players; reminding me the1954 team was state finalist runners-up. Thanks to him also, for sending his resume of accomplishments that include Superintendent of

Calvert ISD and being voted Superintendent of the year in 1994 by Region VI.

Thanks to Shirley I. Knox Barnett for confirming names of teachers at Washington Elementary School and a picture of her father Edward H. Knox, who was principal of Washington Elementary School from 1934-1943.

To James C. Mosley for remembering the valedictorian of the class of 1953; and Amos for confirming the phone number of Melvin Turner.

To Queen Esther Vaults Shaw for professional career information about herself and her sister Vivian Rawls.

To Clyde Ferguson for phone trips we shared down memory lane about former athletes.

To Nettie Richardson Clay who provided names of her classmates who taught public school.

Thanks to Bessie Gibbs Mason for providing the latest phone numbers of her brothers and sisters.

To Willie Taylor who shared phone numbers and memories of E. A. Kemp and Texas Southern University.

Thanks also to "Blues Man" Nat Dove for information about other Kemp Alumni, sharing his many accomplishments, and connecting me with other E.A. Kemp luminaries in music.

They all deserve invaluable credit for their many contributions and have my deep appreciation for their assistance. But, I alone must take credit for any and all errors.

Honor & Recognition

So we stand here
On the edge of hell
In Harlem (Bryan)
And look out on the world
And wonder
What we're gonna do
In the face of
What we remember."
Langston Hughes (Bell 1992, p.15).

This book is written in honor and recognition of all parents and teachers who suffered humiliations, insults, and personal attacks because of their skin color. To parents who bore the pain of wanting more for their children but did not have the means. To parents, especially mothers, who watched their sons go off to fight in wars for freedoms they did not enjoy. To parents who worked long days in the brutally hot Texas sun, picking corn, cotton, and onions, and still could not make ends meet. To mothers, (without cars) who because Bryan did not have a public transit system, had to walk on sore, tired aching feet to and from work. To mothers, again, who worked in the homes of people with much, but paid as little as fifty-cents a day. To a community of citizens who were not allowed to vote because some could not pay a poll tax. For fathers, especially the unskilled with limited education who were not able to support their families and as a result, turned to alcohol to dull their pain, which led to more humiliation and further poverty. To young men who joined the armed forces to escape the restrictions Bryan imposed upon them along with circumstances that thwarted their ability to realize their potential success.

To classmates, who had to wear hand-me-downs and second-hand shoes, who wanted to play in the school band when parents could not afford the instruments. To classmates and neighbors who wanted to participate in Cub and Boy Scouts when parents could not afford to buy uniforms. To all the students who attended Washington Elementary School and given used textbooks. To all the basketball players who had to play on dirt courts, and football players who had to play in used uniforms. But in spite of dirt courts and used uniforms, played like Roman Gladiators. To all those who suffered in silence, hoping for a better day and future for themselves and families. To the men and women who got up everyday and went to low paying, dead-end, demeaning jobs in order to feed their families. To the men and women who had to bring left over food from cafes and homes of people they worked for in order to feed their children. To all the teachers at Washington Elementary, E.A. Kemp Junior-Senior High, George Washington Carver Elementary, E.A. Kemp Senior High and Robert C.(R.C.) Neal Junior High Schools who started boys and girls on their way. They, as did parents, no doubt found themselves often wondering what they were going to do. Langston Hughes's poem about Harlem at the beginning of this section is especially relevant and appropriate, as it personifies the feelings of many in the African-American Community during the period of life and times under consideration.

Table of Contents

List of Appendices

Chapter 1

History and Background

According to the website on the History of Bryan, Texas, it was incorporated as a city in 1872. Bryan Independent School District (ISD) was established in 1877 but the first public school was not open until 1880, and it was for whites. (Farris, 2001-2009, n.p) However, according to the (Brazos County Time Line from 1875-1899, n.p.) in October of 1880 a school with twenty colored students was opened, too. The same date (1880) is given in the Handbook of Texas Online, n.p.) for the first public black school. But, based on the History of Bryan ISD, the Public School for Colored started in1885 and that is the date used in this book.

Some historical background is important and necessary as a common reference point to understanding what living in Bryan, Texas was like for African-Americans. African-American refers to race and is a proper noun. It replaces the word colored and other appellations used when referring to Negro citizens. The word colored was not, with few exceptions, capitalized, though it referred to race. Contrarily, the word white, when referring to race, was almost always a proper noun and capitalized. Please note, the word(s) from quoted documents in this book are expressed as they were at that time, although, it is understood that black, colored and white are not proper nouns when referred to as race. As stated earlier, the total time period of this project is from 1885-1930 and 1931-1971. However, equal emphasis is focused on the period from 1930-1971, the latter four decades. The time periods will be presented partly through historical facts, oral history, recollections and reflections, starting with Bryan Public School for Colored, which was later named Washington Elementary School, located between E.19th and E. 20th Streets, on the corner of Houston Street, and E.A. Kemp Junior-Senior High School originally located between 20th and 21st Streets, on the corner of N. Congress Street. It concludes when E.A. Kemp Senior High School and Stephen F. Austin, were merged when immediate desegregation was ordered by district court. Merging these two schools resulted in Bryan Senior (Vikings) High School, ending the long stony road of school segregation (Farris 2001-2009, n.p.) Prior to 1930, references are made to the first Bryan Public School for whites, built in 1880 and Bryan Public School for Colored, built in 1885. This was roughly nine years (1876) after the Texas State Constitution prescribed "separate but equal" (unequal) instruction for black children (Handbook of Texas Online, n.p.) The school was a two-story frame structure that burned in (1914) about twenty nine years later. It was replaced with a brick structure located between E.19th and E. 20th Streets, as mentioned earlier, on the corner of Houston Street. While the new (1914) brick building must have been an improvement the restrooms were not inside the building. However, inside restrooms were included later with the addition of new classrooms.

Bryan and the schools were decidedly segregated institutions in Brazos County from their beginning and the schools, in essence, remained from 1885-1971 when they were integrated. I will attempt to show how segregation affected African-Americans living in Bryan during this time. Beginning with public schools and in other inescapable areas of life in the city. Just how segregated this city was, at one time, there were three separate schools one each for African-Americans(colored), Mexican-Americans, and Caucasians (whites). Yet, there were Italian-Americans who lived in the same neighborhood with African-Americans. Growing up, I always thought it was strange that their children did not attend the same schools, that is, with African-Americans. Some of the Italian-Americans who lived and or owned businesses in the neighborhoods, were: Jake Cangelosi, Charles Fererri, Nick Dielo, Don Fazzino, Luke Graffizi, Tony Boe Kelley, Sam Lampo, Sam Restivo, Charles and J. Ruffino, Frank Scalin and others. More will be said about these families later.

Sketches of historical facts, recollections and reflections are presented in the sections that follow by a native (Oswell Person) son of the late Mrs. Vivian Peterson whose faith and determination made me strong. It is my hope that African-Americans who lived in Bryan during the 1930's, currently and in some cases, before, will travel memory lane with me as they read each topic and feel a sense of quite peace and grace. Afterall, many of us have learned, what happened in Bryan, was a microcosm of African-American life in the United States of America.

Mrs. Anne Alberson
Teacher, Third Grade

First Grade: Washington Elementary School

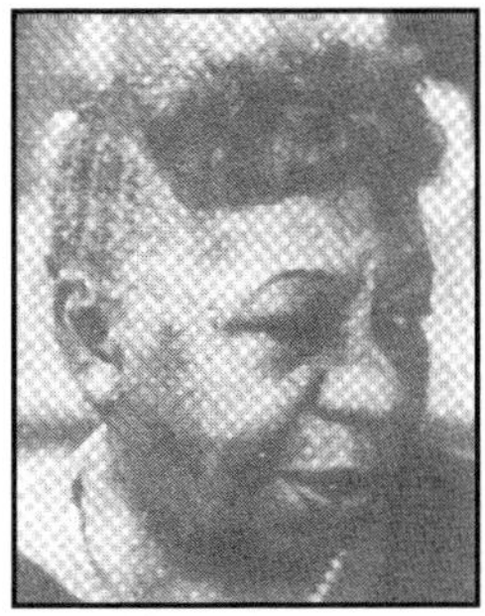

Mrs. Eloise King
Teacher, Music

Before students enrolled in school, vaccinations were required; boys and girls from the Eastside and Westside received their shots on Washington Elementary Campus in a secondary frame building. Having received our shots, armed with Crayons and the revered Big Red Chief Tablet, we were ready for first grade. In addition to indoor plumbing being outside, the school did not have a cafeteria; students had to bring lunch to school. For the most part, many students did not have lunch pales; instead they brought lunch in brown paper bags. In fact, some students did not bring lunch because they were embarrassed. Their parents (mine included) could not afford to buy loaf bread for sandwiches. I was lucky, my classmate Joe W. Toliver, a kid my grandmother used to baby sit and a life-long friend always shared his lunch with me. Plus, his aunt Bernice made hamburgers at the café on the corner of E. 19th Street near Washington School. In Mrs. Doris Scurry's class students had to identify and select food groups from magazines. Then tell classmates which foods they had for breakfast. Many times we would say, "ham and eggs" or "bacon and eggs." The truth was, (I and perhaps others) had corn flakes with water and pet milk. Oftentimes some of us had water and sugar which we called "sweet water" or unpasteurized milk (that came from cows owned by Gertie M. Randle's mother) mixed with left over cornbread or no breakfast at all.

Mrs. Dorris Scurry
Fourth Grade Teacher

When we began first grade the following teachers were at Washington Elementary School: Mrs. Anne Orabel Alberson, Mrs. Irma carter, Mrs. Corine Cass, Mrs. Lelia Hall, Mrs. Eloise King, Mrs. Juanita Martinez, Mrs. Sylvia McIntosh, Mrs. Lorraine Ocheltree, Mrs. Doris Scurry and Ms. Mabel Thomas. Mr. Thomas Cole, Sr. was Principal; he became president of Wiley College later, after leaving Washington School. Teachers who joined the faculty during our attendance were: Mrs. Lula Callier, Mrs. Ella Mae Gregg, Mrs. Hattie Jackson (not related to), Mr. Vernell

Mrs. Lorraine Ocheltree
Fifth Grade Teacher

Mrs. Jessie Mae Walton taught second grade at Washington Elementary School. She taught in the Bryan Public Schools for over 30 years. she was honored as Teacher of the Year in 1977. Mrs. Walton celebrated her 90th birthday on January 1, 2020.

Jackson Mr. Willie Pruitt Ms. Geraldine Toliver and Mrs. Jessie Mae Walton. Mr. Oliver Wayne Sadberry became Principal after Mr. Thomas Cole. The teachers, starting with first-seventh grades were: Mrs. Juanita Martinez, Mrs. Sylvia McIntosh, Mrs. Anne Orabel Alberson, Mrs. Doris Scurry, Mrs. Lorraine Ocheltree, Irma Carter, Mrs. Ella Mae Gregg, Mrs. Lula Callier and Mrs. Eloise King was the music teacher.

Mrs. Fannie Diggs was one of the early teachers at Bryan Public School who became a Principal at Fairview School.

To this day, I remember first names of all my classmates and last names of all but a few who began first grade. They are as follows: Willie Billy Alberson, Luther Baldwin, Luther Bauknite, Andrea Sue Carrol (Lucas), Jo Ann Cole, Homer C. Gillery, Sarah L. Greer Graham, Delores Jean Hall, Fred Hickman, Walter Peter Hollins, Ruben Terrell Jackson, Elmer Lindsay, Jessie Faye Ludd, Marvin?, William Mosley, Shelton Parker, Faye Thelma Patterson, Gloria Patton, Willie B. Perry, Otis Pierce, Robert Ross, Halcyon Sadberry, Opal Jean Sims, Joe W. Toliver, Georgia M. Tramble, Jeanette Walker and Melba Wilson. My classmate Leroy Sterling was the first African-American officially enrolled at Texas A and M University, June 1963 (Texas A and M University Spring 2001, n. p.)

George Washington Carver Elementary School

At the time my classmates and I started school, Washington was the only Elementary School for African-Americans in Bryan. Hence, many of my classmates were from the Westside; we remained together until 1949. In the fall of 1949, children living on the Westside attended George Washington Carver. It was a brand new school that was commonly referred to as Carver for short. All school age children living on the Westside were required to attend Carver. The friendships built with and among Westside students while at Washington were rekindled a few years later in eight grade, at E.A. Kemp Junior-Senior High School.

Mr. Oliver Wayne Sadberry, Principal

In 1949 Mr. Oliver Wayne Sadberry became Principal of Washington Elementary School. He provided excellent leadership for faculty, students and community for over twenty years. In fact, his influence was profoundly felt; not only was he a teacher-principal, he was a mentor and friend. I can still hear him saying "Oswell the world needs finely trained men and women." At the time, I thought that seemed an odd expression but he was trying to prepare us for a future we could not imagine. Another consistent saying of his was "boys and girls don't be mediocre." The last letter I received from him was an offer to come back to Washington and teach. Unfortunately, I could not accept his invitation because I was scheduled to attend graduate school.

As previously mentioned, Bryan Public School for Colored, a frame building, originally burned in 1914 and was replaced with a brick one. The new building was renamed Washington Elementary School after a new school was built on the Westside in 1930 and opened in 1931.(Farris September 30, 2009, n.p.) The new school was E.A. Kemp Junior-Senior High School, named after Mr. Elijah Alonzo Kemp, one of the early principals of Bryan Public School for Colored. In 1929 the Bryan School ISD renamed Bryan High School for whites Stephen F. Austin in honor of the Texas hero. Apparently the student population (1939) grew rapidly, creating the need for a larger school. According to the History of Bryan ISD a new Stephen F. Austin High School was built on 801 S. Ennis Street and remained at that location until court ordered immediate desegregation in 1971.(Farris September 30, 2009, n.p.)

E.A. Kemp Junior-Senior High School

The newly named E.A. Kemp Junior-Senior High School (1930) was reported to have been quite modern although it did not have a gymnasium or cafeteria. The gymnasium built later was a tin barn-like structure with industrial fans instead of air conditioning. None the less, it did provide showers for athletes and physical education students. As I recall no cafeteria was ever added to the 1930 facility. The faculty (some with master's degrees) when we arrived at E.A. Kemp Junior-Senior High School, were: Mrs. Louise Anderson, Mr. Robert Guyden, Mr. James Johnson, Mrs. Willa Johnson, Mr.Willie Moore, Mr. A.K. O'Neal, Mrs. Mell Pruitt, Mr. Claude L. Scurry, Mrs. Sadie Thomas, Mr.Waymon Webster, and Mrs. Johnnie P.Wyatt, Mr. Johnson and Mr.Webster, who earned their Ph.D.'s later and served as university administrators at Prairie View A and M and Texas Southern Universities. Mr. R.C. Neal was Principal and Mrs. Sylvia Sadberry was School Secretary. Some of the others who joined the faculty later, were Mrs. Betty J. Hatchett, Mr. Marion Haynes, Ms. Edessie McClendon, Mr. Hiawatha Webber, Mrs. Freddie Mae Martin Robinson, Mrs. Bernice Webster, Ms. Olivia

Banks, and Mr. Colquitt D. Yancy became principal after Mr. R.C. Neal retired. As stated above, E.A. Kemp High did not have a cafeteria.

However, students and faculty had six places where they could eat. Scott's Diner across the street was where hot lunches were served and many faculty and a few students ate. Campus Inn across the street near the corner of N. Congress Street was the second choice, where hot dogs, hamburgers, chips and sodas were on the menu. Littleton's Snack Bar was a third choice for fast foods such as hot dogs, hamburgers, floats, and French fries. Washington Elementary School did not have a cafeteria when we started school. But Mr. Stearne who owned a grocery store near the campus, let students who otherwise would have gone without buy for ten-fifteen cents, lunch meat, saltines and sodas for lunch. Allowing students to buy lunch this way was an innovative practice that was adopted by other stores. Sam Mosley's Grocery Store, across from Littleton's Snack Bar, was the fourth choice where students could for ten-fifteen-twenty cents buy lunch meat, saltines, chips and sodas. The fifth choice for lunch was Nelson's Café in the same block where faculty and students could enjoy hot meals. The last place was Scanlin's Grocery Store located at the corner of W. 19th and N. Congress Streets where students could buy lunch meat, saltines and sodas the same as they could at Mosley's Store.

E.A. Kemp Senior High School and R.C. Neal Junior High School

Between 1960-61, the total population of Bryan reached over 27,542. (Bryan, Texas 1960 Population, n.p.) The increase in growth created the need for a new high school (1961) for African-Americans; as a result, E.A. Senior High School was built at 1601 W. 19th Street. Unlike the Kemp Junior-Senior built in 1930, the new school had a caféteria and gymnasium. Also, it was the first time senior high students had a campus they did not share with junior high students. (Farris 2001-2009, n.p.) Upon completion of E.A. Kemp Senior High, Bryan had four schools for African-Americans. After the senior high school was built, the former E.A. Kemp Junior-Senior High School was renamed R.C. Neal Junior High. It remained for about nine years under the leadership of the following Principals: Mr. Ulysses S. Morgan, Dr. Wendell Davis, Jr., former student, grid iron, track and field star, and legendary coach of the E.A. Kemp Bears Mr. Claude L. Scurry. Sadly, the school was destroyed by fire but the treasured memories live on. In spite of segregation as way of life, many African-Americans made noteworthy contributions to our communities, among whom were small business owners, professionals, civic leaders, educators and parents. More about these pioneers, and others will be said later.

E.A. Kemp High, Extra-Curricular Activities

Pictured is the 1932 Bryan Colored High School Football Team . Front - far left: Coach Robert Wilson. Far right: Principal, Robert C. Neal

At E.A. Kemp High, boys could participate in all three sports, basketball, football, track and field; girls participated in basketball and track and field. The school's mascot was a Bear, but the athletes played like tigers against competitors in football. The players demonstrated the heroic courage and tenacity in sports that was exemplified by the African-American community in general. Although Kemp was small, it competed against big city teams in Austin, Beaumont, Corpus Christi, Galveston, Port Arthur, San Antonio, and Waco. The schedule also included small city teams in Corsicana, Hearne, Hillsboro, Marlin, Mexia, and Temple. Anderson High Yellow Jackets (Austin) was stiff competition, and had the distinction of having the largest marching band in the conference. Carver High (Waco), Central High (Galveston), Herbert of (Beaumont), Lincoln High (Port Arthur), Phyllis Wheatley (San Antonio) and Solomon Cole (Corpus Christi) were schools, as expected, with superior teams. But the Bears, for the most part, usually faired well in football against the big city teams. Against teams with similar demographics such as Hearne, Marlin and Hillsboro, to name a few, the Bears were generally superior.

The roster of football players consisted of both outstanding and exceptional athletes; some even lettered in all three varsity sports. Starting with Bryan Public School for Colored (1930), predecessor to E.A. Kemp Junior-Senior High School, players like Bruce Barrow, William Cavitt, William Hall, Wesley Hannah, Jethro Hatchett, Dixon McIntosh, Kermit Scott and Finnis Williams filled out the roster. (Buford

Pictured are the Letterman of Football Team, 1947, Coach C.L. Scurry, far left; Principal, R.C. Neal, far right. Some of the players were Joseph Banks, Jr.; Arthur Adams; Romalis Lane; Wendell Davis. The Assistant coach was Willie Moore.

Varsity Basketball Team State Runners-Up of 1965-66. Kneeling - L to R: Horace Jones, Arthur Sandle, James Bailey, Captain: Johnny Williams, and Robert Thorton, Co-Captain. Standind - L to R; Coach C.L. Scurry, Otis Asberry, Billie Amerson, Benjamin Nicks, Otis Carter, James Nixon, Coach Robert Guyden, and Principal W.D. Dunn

n.d.) Dixon McIntosh's, wife Sylvia McIntosh (mentioned earlier) was my second grade teacher; Kermit Scott was a relative of the Hollywood personality Bob Scott who was in the 1948 movie"Look Out Sister" with Louis Jordan. Some of the football players in the 1940's, who followed the 1930's teams and lettered in basketball(B) football (FT) or track and field (TF) were: Arthur Adams (FT), Bill Albright (FT), Jody Banks (FT), James Boone (FT), Ralph Campbell (FT), Sloan Clopton (FT), Edward L. Colquitt (FT), Wendell Davis (B-FT-TF), Robert Graves (FT), Robert Green (FT), Clifton Greer (FT), James (Jim) Greer (FT), James Hill (FT), Romalis Lane (FT), Walter Patton (FT), Felix Petty (FT), Charlie Sanders (FT), Joe Wille Toliver * (FT), Hiawatha Webber (FT), Otha White (FT) Collie Williams, (FT) Marion "Buck" Williams (FT) and Marion Haynes (TF). Clifton Greer moved to San Francisco in 1945 where he still resides.* His brother James Greer, who also played in the1940's, lives in Oakland, CA.* Dr.Wendell Davis who died in September 2009, was captain of the 1948 squad and Edward L. Colquitt,* who was co-captain, lives in Richmond, California currently. Wendell Davis was also an exceptional track star who set an unbroken record for running the fastest 100 meters and participated in the Olympic trials. Joe Willie Toliver* retired as a Captain on the Seattle, Washington Police Force and lives in the city. Marion "Buck" Williams* lived in New York for years but came back home, operated a barber shop and lives in Bryan.

The teams in 1950-59 continued a tradition established in the 1930's and 1940's; the roster of talented players some of whom participated in basket ball (B), football (FT), track and field (TF) are listed below:

Davis Edwards (FT)
H.P. "Frock" Emanuel (B)
Rastine "Foxall" Jones (FT)
William Hughes (FT)

Fred Douglas Lewis (B-FT-TF) outstanding
R.C. "Bucket" Wallace (B)
Charles Murphy (FT)
Ernest Brown (FT)

Homer Rice (FT)
John Steen (FT)
John Dunn (B-FT)
Harrell Johnson (B-FT)
Arthur Brown (FT)
Roosevelt "Joe" Owens (FT)
Nathaniel "Nick" Allen (FT)
Johnny Ellis (TF)
Clyde Ferguson (FT)
Clarence "Boe" Stephney (TF)
Roger Turner (TF)
Issac "Long John" Watson (TF)
Rastine Calhoun (FT)
Clifton "Bubba" Holland (B-FT-TF)
Lorenzo Scurry (FT-TF)
Tommy"Trigger" Traylor (FT-TF)
Hiriam Henley (TF)
John D. White (FT)
Samuel Dunn (FT)
Billy Ray Smith (B-FT)
George Bell (FT)
Lawrence Ellis (TF)
David Littleton (FT)
James "Dooley" Martin (FT-TF)
O.D. Baker (FT)
Larry Nutall (B-FT)
Raymond Moore (TF)
Jackie Sims (TF)
Lloyd Williams (B-FT)
Milton Elarms (B)
William D. Hollins (FT)
James Sheppard, Jr. (B-FT-TF)
William Robert Stewart (FT)
Ray Steen (FT)
Curtis Miles (FT)
Lawrence "Big Boy" Nutall (FT)
Ennis "Pete" Owens (FT)
Amos L. White (FT)
Arthur Dunn (B-FT)
Robert Louis Smith (B-FT)
Willie S. Mitchell (FT)
Melvin Turner (B-FT)
George Vaults (B)
Joseph G. Williams (FT)
Dennis Garner (FT)
Frank Perry, Jr. (B)
Willie C. Smith (FT)
John L. Williams (FT-TF)
Oscar Johnson (FT-TF)
Isiah Phillips (FT-TF)
William Dunn (B-FT)
Daniel C. Banks (FT)
Howard Duren (FT)
Elmaurice Harris (B)
James H. Littleton (FT)
Charles Sterling (FT)
Jon Allen Mosley (FT)
Cloyd "Flip" Williams (FT)
Oscar Webb (TF)
James Turner (TF)
Andrew Byrd (FT)
Bobby Joe Hill (B)
Elliott Myers (FT)
Quinton Walton, Jr. (B)

From 1960-1971 the tradition of outstanding athletes at Kemp continued until a court order in 1971 ended segregation and E. A. Kemp High and Stephen F. Austin merged into Bryan (Vikings) Senior High School. The roster before the merger consisted of individuals who lettered (commonly) in basketball (B), football (FT) and track and field (TF). The following list of players is incomplete but representative of the talent that was perennial for the E. A. Kemp Bears, players included:

Players on the E.A. Kemp 1953-54 Basketball Team were State Runners-Up. First row front: Luther Baldwin - trainer. Second row: L to R - Lloyd Walker. Harrell Johnson, Frank Perry, Jr.; Melvin Turner, Third row: L to R - Unknown, Unknown, Unknown, George Vaults, Billy Ray smith, Top row: L to R - Unknown, Clifton Holland

James Herman Alberson (B-TF)
Curtis Dix (FT)
William G. Hall (B-FT)
Sam Jackson (B-FT)
Frank Jones (FT)
Bobby Joe Perry (B-FT)
Lloyd Suseberry (FT-TF)
Charles Benford (FT)
Lucious Bisor (FT),
Douglas Carter (FT),
Elton Coleman (B)
J.C. Davis (B)
Charles Nelson (FT-TF)
Hayward Peterson (FT)
Albert Sims (FT),
Wilford Walton (B-FT)
Billy Chambers (B)
Green (FT) John
William Warren (FT)
Charles Childs (FT)
Leroy Cunningham (B)
Otis Asberry (B-FT)
William Bell (B-FT)
Jerry Cook (FT-TF)
Merion Ellis (FT-TF)
James Irvin (FT)
Benjamin Nicks (TF)
Arthur (Boe) Sandle (B-FT)
Jerry W. Sweeps (FT)
James Watson (F)
Clarence Thomas (FT)
James Bailey (B)
Otis Carter (B-FT)
Claude Ellis (B)
Robert Green (B-FT-TF)
John Latson (FT)
Waymon Peterson (FT)
Thomas Shields (FT)
Robert Thornton (B)
Johnny Williams (B)

The basketball teams won district championships in the 1950's and 1960's under the legendary leadership of Head Coach Claude L. Scurry, and Head Coach Bobby Joe Perry, a former player for Coach Scurry. The girls played a half court style of basketball earlier. Although they played a different style of basketball, they were very good. In fact, some were outstanding. Team members included: Juanita "Pap" Carter,+* resides in Houston, Mildred Tramble+, Shirley Knox, Ester Ruth Bradley, Doris Green Coleman+*, lived in Portland for years but now resides in Bryan, Ernestine Bradley, Mildred Hughes, Anne R. Johnson, Geraldine Adams,+* lives in Oakland, California, Eva Lois Allen, Beatrice Bradley, Emmaline Gause, Pearl Ester Murkledove, Mary A. Smith, Sandra L. Nicks, Margie Holloway, Nettie Heads, Erma Faye Hedge, Robbie Hill, Shirley Holland, Dorothy Lewis, Mary C. Myers* lives in L.A., Mary L. Norwood, Carolyn Peterson, Barbara Richardson, Nettie E. Thurman* lives in Bryan, Mineola Vaults* resides in Pacoima, California, Qweda Caldwell* lives in Beaumont, Novella Gaffford* lives in Dallas, Gloria Knox, Rudell Moore, Annette Norwood, Lilly Norwood and Ernestine Wilson. As was stated above, all the girls were good but based on my imperfect memory, I think the ones with plus signs rated above outstanding.

As for the girls' track and field, Billie J. Turner and Doris Green were the standout runners, I can remember. The boy's track and field teams were as good, if not better than, many of the competing schools. Some of the outstanding members, were Marion Haynes*, Johnny Ellis* (both live in Bryan), Clarence "Bo" Stephney (deceased), and Roger Turner* (retired from the US Army) and lives in Lawton, Oklahoma and Issac"Long John"Watson. Johnny Ellis and Marion Haynes ran the 100 meters, Clarence Stephney, Roger Turner and Issac "Long John" Watson were long distance runners. Baseball as a team sport was added later; some of the players included Horace Jones, Roland Koontz, Leon Murphy, Benjamin Nicks, Robert Person, Ernest Scott and Charles Williams. Some of the many talented boys who received athletic scholarships from 1948-1960 were: Wendell Davis, Robert Ellis, Sloan Clopton, Marion Haynes, Edward L. Colquitt, Joe Willie Toliver, Marion Williams, George Vaults, Clifton Holland, Frank Perry, Lorenzo Scurry, Tommy Traylor an outstanding quarter-back, who in a 1954 game against Booker T. Washington of Dallas ran a kick-off return the length of the field, Lorenzo Scurry, John L. Williams, Elmaurice Harris, Lloyd Williams, Bobby Hill, arguably the best basketball player, in memory, from Brazos County, William G. Hall, lives in Calvert, Texas, and Bobby Joe Perry who lives in Bryan.* In addition to individual and team sports E.A. Kemp had a marching band, cheerleaders, drill team and an outstanding choir and majorettes. The band and cheerleaders provided moral support and encouraged the teams to victory. They played a valuable role in promoting school spirit; pride, and unity. Some members of the band, choir, cheerleaders, drill teams, and majorettes are listed below.

Band

Juree Shivers	Oscar Lee Morgan	Coakey E. Carroll
Billy Walker	Herman O. Brown	Robert J. Shields
Fred G. Smith	Mazie Nell Smith	Samuel Smith

William Smith
Ennis Green
John J. Knox
Collie Sanders
Rozell Quarles
Billy R. Smith
Joe W. Toliver
Horace Nelson
Floyd Johnson
Charles Pharms
Joyce King
Donald Childs
Donald R. Johnson
Jurline Wilson
Clifton Holland
James T. Murphy
Lorenzo Scurry
Jimmy L. Tillery
Fred Hickman
James Turner
Nathaniel Dove (Nat)
Sylvester Lewis
Janice Thurman
Melvin Littleton
Charles Watson
Albert Griffin
Leon Davis
Edward H. Knox, Jr.
Ina Richardson
Willie C. Smith
Alyce Tyler
Sidney Simpson
Shirley Holland
Etta Duren
Lonnie Mulkey
Marion Jones
James Alberson
Weldon Walton

A Cappella Choir

Billy Alberson
Samuel Callier
Bessie Gibbs
Georgia Kennard
Lorenzo Scurry
Willie C. Smith
Cloyd Williams
Luther Baldwin
Etta Duren
Dorothy Green
Gloria Knox
Darlene Sheppard
Walter Sterling
John L. Williams
Rastine Calhoun
Charles E. Ellis
Gladys Green
Ina Richardson
Opal Sims
John D. White

Cheerleaders

Top: Sheryl Shivers
Left: Joan Robertson
Right: Ruby Newton
Left: Patricia Brown
Right: Sandra Alexander
Kneeling: Mildred Ray

Lela Mae Burton

Ruby Lois Greene

Erma Faye Goffrey

Erma F. Goffney
Margie Holloway
Doris Green
Clarence Stephney
Laura J. Ward
Lela Burton
Frank Perry
Sandra Alexander
Lorenza Shirley
Annie R. Johnson
Emmaline Gause
Ruby L. Green
Alyce Tyler
Patricia Brown

Ruby Newton
Sheryl Shivers
Mildred Ray
Joan Robinson

Drill Squad (Team)

Ruby Lois Greene

Johnnie Patterson

Iona Potts

Ina Richardson

Ruby Green
Johnnie Patterson
Amy L. Bradley
Erma Goffney
Iona Potts
Mary A. Lewis
Lanetta Hollins
Ina Richardson

Majorettes

Alice Joyce Tyler

Eva Lois Harrison

Eva Lois Harrison
Doris Mcrae
Irene Bradley
Shirley Chambers
Maxine Morris
Doris Thompson
Lorraine Sterling
Carolyn King
Charlie M. Davis
Barbara R. Calhoun
Blossie T. Philips
Gwendolyn Stearne
Jo Floy Shirley
Doris J. Ford
Bessie Gibbs
Era Whitehead
Darlene Sheppard
Peggy Humphrey
Erma J. Hawkins
Tina B. Sims
Ray Watson
Georgia Johnson
Melvin J. Traylor
Dorothy J. Banks
Georgia Tramble
Melba Moore

Other, not all, clubs and organizations that gave students a chance to demonstrate their abilities, and talents, included, Dramatic Arts; Hi-Y, Jets, Leadership, Lettermen's Club, Performing Arts (Jazz Band), and Tri-Y Clubs. Two of the several student organizations, included the Student Council, and the National Honor Society. Adolph Johnson, Jr., Mildred Ray, Linda Smith and Marva Wilson were charter members of the National Honor Society.

Performing Arts-Jazz Band

As mentioned above under extra-curricular activities, E.A. Kemp had many talented student musicians. In the 1950's and 1960's the student musicians came

E. A. Kemp High Band under the direction of Mr. Waymon Webster in the 1950's. Left to Right: D. Hollins, J. Toliver, W. Taylor, R. Jackson, H. Nelson, R. Quarles, M. Jones, J.J. Knox, J.H. Alberson, C. Pharms, E. Knox, M. Littleton, J. King, J. Thurman, S. Lewis, I. Richardson, A. Tyler, F. Hickman, J. Turner, N. Dove, F. Johnson, E. Duren, S. Simpson, E. Green and R. Ross.

under the influence and tutelage of band directors Mr. Hardy Ray Murphy, Dr. Waymon Webster and Mr. A.C. Shead. Of the three band directors, Waymon Webster had the greatest impact on the aspirations and careers of the up and coming young musicians. Dr. Webster was more than the typical band director in that he helped the student see into the future by raising their horizons beyond Bryan. Furthermore, he set himself apart from other band directors by teaching music harmony, theory, conducting, orchestration and music arranging. One of his former students, Nathaniel Dove paid special honor to Dr. Webster presenting him the Bakersfield Blues Preservation Society Plaque in 2006. Some of the young students whose music development was nurtured by Dr. Webster, affectionately known as Jack, who became professional musicians are as follows: Fred G. Smith, Lorenzo "Bunny" Scurry, Nathaniel "Nat" Dove, Marion "Boddie" Jones, Donald "Dickie" Childs, Albert Griffin, Donald Ray Johnson and Clyde Dove, Nate's brother.

1960 Band Members, Mr. C.A. Shead, Director

Many of these musicians further honed their skills in local night spots in Bryan and other venues in Texas. Some left Bryan and played in cities and states like Albuquerque, New Mexico, Las Vegas, Nevada, Los Angeles and San Francisco.

Student life at E. A. Kemp High was not about study only. Pictured are two choirs in the 1950's and 1960's. The choirs were comprised of students with great musical talent and voices. Under the direction of Mrs. Johnnie Wyatt the choir was rated superior annually.

The musicians who played in venues in the United States only are listed in alphabetical order below. Donald "Dickie" Childs a saxophonist, played in clubs and other venues in Texas; and attended the University of North Texas (formerly North Texas State). Clyde Dove played in and around Bryan before leaving for California. During the time he played piano in local clubs: He was all Blues. Since moving to California he has switched his talents to Gospel Music. Clyde currently resides in Inglewood, California. Albert Griffin as he was known at E.A. Kemp (now Damu Sudi Ali) is a pianist. He is proficient in blues, classical, and top forty, but as he says "Jazz is his bread and butter." Damu has for the past eight years been a regular at the Lazy Lees Jazz Bistro in San Francisco. He has a CD of original compositions and is soon to release a new C D with his son Jabari Ali. Damu also played with the Umoja Band, attended Texas A and M University and Laney College, and teaches music at private middle school in Oakland, California. Marion Jones was a tremendously gifted saxophonist from E. A. Kemp who attended the University of North Texas where he was a member of one of the renowned Jazz Lab Bands. He too played night spots in and around Bryan and other venues in Texas until relocating to Los Angeles where he became a Hollywood Studio Musician. Lorenzo "Bunny" Scurry was arguably the best trumpet player ever to come out of E.A. Kemp. He was a regular in night clubs in Las Vegas for many years.

Nat Dove in Concert at Chochi, Japan circa 2001

Still a few E. A. Kemp Alumni lived and played in Belgium, Canada, Paris, France and Tokyo, Japan. The three musicians who took their music to worldwide concert halls and Jazz Festivals are: Fred G. Smith another very gifted saxophonist, according to his teacher, with perfect pitch. As a high school student his sounds were comparable to the likes of Charlie Byrd, Paul Desmond, Dexter Gordon and Sonny Rollins. Fred played in night clubs in the Bryan and cities in the state of Texas. He attended Graduate Schools of Music at the Universities of Texas and North Texas State. Fred formed a Fred Gene Combo while attending graduate school and played in the big cities of Texas before moving to California in 1969. Fred wrote and arranged music for Smokey Robinson. In fact, he wrote one his songs, "Quiet Storm," while with the legendary Smokey Robinson Group. He played with the late Ray Charles' Orchestra and toured the United States and world.

Donald Ray Johnson is a gifted Blues drummer and vocalist influenced by Dr. Webster; he has played in the states and concert halls and Jazz Festivals in Belgium, Canada, France and Switzerland. Donald is an International Recording Artist with releases in 1998, 2002 and 2006. I had the pleasure of meeting and talking by phone with Donald while he was playing a Jazz Festival in France on March 24, 2010. Donald won a Grammy in 1979 while playing with a group called the Taste of Honey. He was voted best male Blues vocalist in 2007 by Real Blues Magazine; and was winner of the 2008 Blewzzy Award. Donald's many credits and musical contributions are listed on his website *www.donaldrayjohnson.com*. Donald is based in Calgary, Canada where he has lived for about twenty years and holds dual citizenship in Canada and the United States.

Nathaniel "Nat" Dove is the last of the above group who was a student of Dr. Webster. He, too, started as a little boy trying to play the family piano and now is considered the quintessential Bluesman in the business today. His list of contributions, credits, recordings and educational accomplishments are beyond the pages allocated in this chapter. However, some highlights are critical and are indicated below. Dove's or Nat's (as he is known in entertainment) credits include arranging, composing, producing and performing with many of the Great Blues Personalities in America. He has played, traveled throughout the world and lived in Paris, France and Tokyo, Japan. He founded the Bakersfield Blues Preservation Society to promote Blues music as an art form through education. Some activities of the Society include Blues Alive a Radio Show and Blues In the Schools Program. While living and working in Paris, he composed the musical score for the critically acclaimed play, "Sail to Everest." Dove studied Music Business at Columbia College, Music Broadcast Communication at L.A. City College, Film Music at UCLA and Music Composition at New York University. One of Dove's Recordings: "The Most Requested Rhythm Band" sold 750,000 copies. For a comprehensive view of Dove's range of talents and work see his websites: *www.natedove.com* and *www.boogiebluesconnection.com.* Dove and his fellow musicians are again evidence that students from E.A. Kemp did indeed Move Forward From Behind.

Mrs. Johnnie P. Wyatt E.A. Kemp's legendary music teacher and choir director was famous for the prize winning A Cappella Choir. One of her students, Franks Perry, Jr. studied at the renowned Julliard School of Music. Another student of hers, Sterling Williams (Walter L. Sterling as he was known at Kemp) is a successful Blues recording Artist. Sterling has lived in Chicago, Detroit and played throughout the United States and resides in Los Angeles currently. He on the list of Soul Blues Artists and appears on 21st Century Blues. His top albums are "Brand New Man, Grade A Quality and My Baby's Love." For more detail about Sterling Williams see *www.soulbluesmusic.com.*

***Note: address information is based on the 1990 E.A. Kemp High Class Reunion Directory, Bryan ISD Directory 2002 and personal interviews.**

Chapter 2

"However Tall the Mountain There's A Road." – Afghanistan

E.A. Kemp High School Alumni:
Academic and Professional Achievement

Alma Mater Dearest
We love and cherish, memories of you-only you.
Hearts forever loyal to you, so royal our alma mater.
So will you, dear Kemp High,
Always inspire, guide and lead your sons and daughters,
Give us consolation and inspiration
We love you, Kemp High- Kemp High School

Music - Hardy Ray Murphy and Words – J.L Wyatt

Given the humble living conditions, separate and "unequal" educational opportunities, many sons and daughters of E.A. Kemp Junior-Senior and Senior High Schools earned bachelors, masters, doctoral and professional degrees in education, dentistry, law, medicine, pharmacy, social work and theology. In spite of limited resources, segregation, and not being able to reach their potential, students demonstrated again and again they could excel, as you will read below and later in the section on **Public Schools, Government, Higher Education and Private Sector**. Rather than being crippled or defeated by the social conditions of an uneven society students were emboldened. The names of valedictorians, and students who earned degrees, and the institutions they attended, reads like "Who's Who." Their names, and where known, specific degrees are noted. Otherwise, B is for Bachelor and M for Master, and institutions they attended are listed below.

Edward H. Knox, Sr.-BS
John T. Lane-M
Blanche Barrow-B
Edna Harris Tarrow-M

Johnnie L. P. Wyatt-B
Irene Randle Lane-M*
Lawrence King- M
Odis T. Walton-B
Richard Dix-B
Jessie Mae Hunter Walton-M.Ed
Doris Stearne Scurry-M
Lolethia Stearne-B
Chanie Dix-B
Bethenia Ellis Wallace-M*
Carolyn Beatrice Hammond-MD
Beatrice Potts Scott-M*
W.C. Daniels-B
Maggie Sheppard-M
William A. Hammond, Jr.-MD
Ruth Neal-M
Esterline Moore-B
Lovie Jewell Hammond-JD
Zack Grays-M
Martha Potts-M
Freddie Mae Martin-M
Ella Mae Groce-M
Pearlie Prunella Petty-M
Irene Shields Mitchell-B
Betty Jean Holland-B
Catherine Martin-Ph.D.
Dorelia Powell Taylor-M
Gladys Sanders Wallace-M
Mary Frances Bradley-M
Rosa L. Rouse Edwards-B
Robert J. Shields-M
Tommie Mae Dabney-M
Arthur Dunn-B
Doris Green Coleman-B
Jesse Rhone-B
Fred G. Smith-B
Frankie Morris-B
George Vaults-M-M
Fannie Herdon Diggs-M
Lawrence King-M
Tommie Mae Murphy-M
Ulysses Wallace-B
Wendell C. Davis, Jr.-Ed.D.
Rosie Mae Rice Greer-M
Charles Hammond-DDS
Cora Hall Tennant-M
Darcus Lightfoot*
Merion Haynes-B
Alberta Biggers Knox-BS
Hiwatha Webber-B
Edward L. Colquitt-B
Alandrus Peterson, Jr.-MS (1937)
Vivian Murphy Duren-BSN
Bettye J.D. Hatchett-M
Thelma Moore-B
Coakey Ellsworth Caroll-B
Lorraine Sterling-M
Betsy Brown-Ph.D.
Imogene Petty Johnson-M
Wauline Pierce Gamble-Ed.D
Andrew Truman Daniel-B
James Lightfoot-DD
Daisy Ray Hollins*
Davis Edwards-B
Shirley I. Knox-BSN
James C. Mosley-BS
Martha Miller-B
Mazy Nell Smith Mack-M*
Amos L. White-BS
Doris Mae Dix-M
Clyde Ferguson-MSW
Blossie T. Phillips-M
Melvin Turner-B+
Tommie Mae Dabney-M
John Jerome Knox-M*
Samuel Callier-MDiv

Esterline Allen-BS
Ann E. King-MS
James T. Murphy-B
Frank Perry-DA
Iona Potts-M
John L. Williams-M
Royce Pace-BS
Darlene Sheppard Abrams-Ed.D.
James Knox-BS, R.Ph.
Willie Alberson-BS
Wanda Jackson-M
Dearest Mack-B
Milton Green-BA
David Littleton-B
Faye Patterson Sabbs-M
Leroy Sterling-M
Joe Willard Toliver-Ph.D.
Ben Adams-B
Etta J. Duren-M (HS)
Vivian Faye Littleton-M
Raymond Moore-M
James Sterling-MS (HS)
Ethel Twitty-B
Andrew Byrd, Jr.-M
Iney Cunningham-M
Fred L. Jefferson-B
Clarence Mack-B
Mildred L. Ross Phillips-B
Elmira Toines-BSN
Opal Jewel Turner-B
Curtis Dix-B
James Herman Alberson-B
Bobby Joe Perry-M
Betty Suseberry-M
Barbara King-B
Hayward Peterson-B
Odis Walton, Jr., JD
John Green-BS
Ruby Dix-MA
Katha Robertson-M
Gladys Nell Green Smith-MSN
Georgia Ann Kennard-BSN
Edna Jones-BSN*
Willie C. Smith-B
Billy Ray Smith-M
Era Whitfield-BS
Luther Baldwin-MBA*
Juanita Gibbs Johnson-BA
Louise Dix-MA
Walter Peter Hollins-MS
James E. Martin-B
Halcyon Sadberry Watkins-DVM
Oswell Person-Ph.D.
O. D. Baker-M.Th-M.Ed.
Melvin Johnson-HS
James M. Allen-B
Frederick D. Knox-BS- R.Ph. (HS)
Ona Johnson Sims-M
Lonnie Mulkey-M
Janice J. Thurman-B
Henry Allen-BS (1960)
Waldo Harnsberry-B
Bobbie Jean Idlebird-B
Gloria Knox-BS
Mildred Monroe-B
Curtis Taylor-B
Thelma Traylor Dove-MSN
Nero Davis-B
William G. Hall-M
Robert Bisor-B
Winston Harnesberry-B
Barbara Bisor-B
Johnnie Mae Moten-M
Albert Sims-JD
Weldon Walton-Ph.D.
Woodrow Jackson-M

Barbara Williams Dixon-MS
Jesse Marvin Walker-BS
Effie Allen Perry-M
Lucille Allen-B
Jo Ann Robinson-B
Eddie Mae Phillips-M
Ruby J.Butler-Ph.D.
Curtis Foley, Jr., MD
Ivy R. Idlebird-B
Maxine Idlebird-B
Tommy L. Green-B
Sharon M. Turner-B
Linda Smith Asbury-M (NHS)
Pearl Collins-M
Sid Garner-Ph.D.
Adolph Johnson, Jr., Ph.D. (NHS)
John Latson-B
Milton Nowlin-B
Calvin Phillips-Ph.D.#
Mildred Ray-M (NHS)
Booker T. Davenport-B
Queen Esther Vaults-B
Charles Wallace-B
Alandrus A. Peterson, Jr.-BS
Claudette Scurry-M
Jerry Guyden-Ph.D.
Lennie Bailey-B
Gwendolyn Thomas-Ph.D.
Waylon Garner-B
Helen McDowell-B
Lloyd Thomas-B
Freddie Thomas-MD
Linda Cunningham-B
Willie Davenport-B
Roy Paul-B
Henry Robertson-JD
Jesse Monroe-B
Vivian Vaults Rawls-B
William Baldwin-BBA
Lillian Johnson-BSN*
Irma Jean Walton-B
George Mitchell-B
Pansy Taylor-B
Anderson Tennell-B
Wanda Peterson Green-M
Carolyn Sheppard-M-M
Maxie Taylor-B
Nancy Bisor-B
Merion Ellis-BS
James Irvin-B
Andrew Konx-BS
Jo Ann Stephney Jordan-MA
Benjamin Nicks-B
Robert Person-M
Beverley Sheppard-MM (HR)
Karen Walton-B
Marva Wilson-B (NHS)
Hilda Shivers-B
Cheryl Shivers-B
Garfield Scott-B (1960)
Robert Guyden-M
Gwendolyn Davis-M
Lorenzo Scurry-B
Rose Cowan-B
Lynda Green-BS
Eddie Smith-B
Marilyn Jones-B
Willie Allen-B
Clovis Pruitt-M
Cheryl Banks-B
James Davis-B
Agnes Goins-B
William Walton-B
Claddie McNeal-B
Cecil Webster-M(@)
Willie Pruitt-M(@)

John D. White* (1954)
Nora Allen-BSN (1960)
Billy Cunningham-BS (1960)
Johnny Wesley Jordan-BS (1965)
Johnny Robertson-B
Altha Smith-M (1967)

*Valedictorian
Transferred to Stephen F. Austin Senior Year
NSH-National Honor Society
HR- Honor Roll
@Transferred to Bryan High
(HS) Honor Student

Still other E. A. Kemp Alumni continued their education by attending such institutions as The American Banking Institute, Aspen Institute, Business, Technical-Trade Schools, Heavy Equipment School and numerous four-year and two-year colleges. They earned associate degrees, certificates, professional certifications and licensure required to practice in their respective professions, such as Finance, Management and Nursing, to name a few. Their accomplishments demonstrate in the same way as the individuals mentioned above that they could move forward from behind and achieve when given access and opportunity. The names of many of the individuals, but not all, and the institutions they attended are listed below.

Hardie Allen
Arthur K. Brown
Andrea S. Carroll
Lorenzo Davis
Willie D. Finley
Leroy Gibbs
Sam Jackson
Jessie R. Jefferson
Edward H. Knox, Jr.
Lovie J. Littleton
Ernest Moore
Isaiah Phillips
Earline Phillips
James Sheppard, Jr.
Robert Smith
Paul Toliver
Mineola Vaults
Velma Polk Allen
Herman O. Brown
Nettie R. Clay
Johnny Ellis
Howard Gibbs
James A. Green
Jesse J. Jefferson
Autry E. Jones
Erie Lovell Knox
Ollie R. Martin
Robert Newman
James Ray
Conchita Sadberry
Jackie Sims
Clarence Stephney
Searcy Toliver
Velma Vaults
Margaret Gibbs Brooks
Rastine Calhoun
James Cooper
Ruby Green Ellis
James O. Gibbs
James Harnsberry
Sam Jackson
Carolynne King
James Littleton
Mary G. McClain
Jeffrey Nutall Moore
Tarryline Richardson
Collie Sanders
Sidney E. Simpson
Charles Sterling
Geraldine Vaults
John D. White

Erthel Wooley
Sarah Greer Graham*
Leon Davis*
Grace King*
Mary Frances Taylor*
Albert Griffin*
Waymon T. Peterson*
Barbara Wright
Barbara J. Rucker*
Tommie J. Duren*
Jon Allen Mosley*
Nathaniel Dove
Donald Ray Johnson*
Ethel Batten*
Tommie D. Duren*
Margaret R. Rucker
Minerva Potts Smith*
Brenda Patterson*
Donald Childs*
Charles Nelson*

* Late entries

Institutions Alumni Attended

E.A. Kemp Alumni attended and earned their degrees from colleges and universities in the Midwest, North, South and West. The institutions are arranged in alphabetical order as follows: American Institute of Banking, American University (DC), Antioch College (Ohio), The Aspen Institute, Bishop College, Boston University, California State University Dominguez Hills, California State University Hayward, California State University, Sacramento, City College of San Francisco, Clark-Atlanta University, Columbia University, Cornell University, Draughn's Business College, Fisk University, Gammon Theological Seminary, General Motors Institute (Michigan), Hampton University, Houston Business College, Houston Community College, Howard University, Humboldt State University (CA), Hunter College (New York), Huston-Tillotson (Austin) Jarvis Christian College, Julliard School of Music, Laney College (Oakland, CA) Lewis and Clark University (Ore), Lincoln University (PA), Los Angeles City College, Metropolitan State College (Denver), Michigan State University, Milwaukee County Institutions, Mortuary Science College, Mountain View Community College, Northern Baptist Theological Seminary, Paul Quinn College, Pepperdine University (CA), Prairie View A and M University, Prince George's Community College, Princeton University, San Francisco State University, Saint Mary's College of Nursing (Arizona), Saint Mary's University (San Antonio), Saint Philips College (San Antonio), Southern University, (La), Texas A and M University (College Station), Texas A and M University Annex, Texas College, Texas Southern University, Texas Woman's University, United States Naval Academy, University of California (Berkley), University of California (LA), University of California (Santa Barbara), University of Chicago, University of Houston, University of Maryland, University of Northern Colorado, University of the Pacific, University of Southern California, University of Texas, Virginia Polytechnic State University, West Point Military Academy, Wilberforce University, Wiley College, Woodbury University and Yale University.

Chapter 3

Employment Opportunities: Jobs (Private)

Education was not the only separate and unequal opportunity for African-Americans living in the city of Bryan; employment was too. According the web-site, "Bryan is a promising, thriving, forward looking city." This was not the case for early African-American residents. They faced limited and restricted employment chances, along with other mind numbing experiences. In general, most African-Americans, with few exceptions, were relegated to the bottom of the job well. They worked the dead-end, custodial, menial and pitifully low paying jobs. Exceptions to this rule may have been drivers for private van line companies, telephone operators, chefs (head cooks) and Lilly Ice Cream workers. All together the exceptions would only account for a small percentage of individuals who were not employed in low paying menial type jobs. For example, Clarence Harris, Essay McCoy, John McGee, Joe Perry and Clarence Stephney (van line drivers), John Knox (Lilly Ice Cream Company employee), Brenda Patterson and Ernestine Richards (telephone employees) are a few of the individuals who may have earned a decent wage. The US Post Office, although not the private sector, employed African-Americans to clean the building and polish brass. The exception came when LaRue Johnson, Ples Turner, Odis Walton, Sr. and Savannah Smith Williams (WW-II Veterans) were hired as mail carriers. Re-activation of Bryan Air Base in 1951 afforded some jobs but did not change the situation appreciably. My guess is the few men who were employed on the base earned a decent wage. Ocie Hall, Sr. was one of the few individuals employed at the Base.

Robert Green and Otis Johnson were (top cooks) at the Charles and LaSalle hotels and presumably made good salaries? However, William Allen and Searcy Wilburn who were bell-hops earned very little pay. James Sheppard, Sr. and Willie White were also top cooks, and it is assumed they were remunerated accordingly. Arthur Adams was employed at the First National Bank, Jack Green and Willis E. Ray were employed at Roman's Pharmacy; Peter Davis and Fred Smith were employed at Vick's Pharmacy; Leola Whitehead and Charlie "Womby" were employed at the Palace Theater and Walter Hollins, Sr. was the human elevator among other jobs at the Bryan Hospital. Some of the numerous private businesses and companies that provided employment are/were as follows: Parker-Astin, Borden Milk Company, R.B. Butler, Inc., Cade Motor Company, Caldwell Jewelers, Coca Cola, Corbusier Chevrolet, Dishman Pontiac, Fabricare Laundry and Cleaners, Fashion Cleaners, Food Town Market, Haswell Motor Company, Holick Boot Company, Howell Lumber Company, Humpty Dumpty Market, Kelley's Café-Restaurant, Kraft Furniture Store, Major's Café Restaurant, Meat Locker Plant, McCullough Dansby Furniture, Palace Theater, Parker Lumber Company, Dr. Pepper Bottling Company, Roman's Pharmacy, Sanderson Farms, Seven-Up Bottling Company, Sanitary Farm Dairies, Sugar N Spice Drive Inn, Texas A and M University, Triangle Drive Inn, Varisco Lumber Company,Vick's Pharmacy, A&M Waldrop Clothiers and Woodson Lumber Company. Private homes were another source of employment, primarily for African-American Women. Simply put, as stated earlier, employment was another challenging barrier.

(Public)

The city of Bryan hired African-Americans for menial jobs, at first, as evidenced by two men, Roger Harris and Jim Day, hired to clean dry toilets. Maurice Green Sr., Eddie Phillips, George Banks and Joseph Dove worked on the sanitation trucks. Nathan McGee, Ollie Nelms, Roland Koontz and James "Sunny" Nash drove trash trucks; Terrence Bazy drove the brush truck. Maurice Green started his career with the city as a trash collector but retired as a supervisor after forty-five years of service. Other men worked for the city in different departments, Ennis Owens and David Parker in the Water Department; Horace Nelson, Sr., J.D. Ray and Dave Woods were in the Street Department. Olin Jenkins, and Horace Patterson were in the Water Department. Willie Idlebird and Johnny Brown were the first African-American police officers hired by the city of Bryan. However, when hired they could only arrest their "kind," meaning other African-Americans, only. Two of the several other officers who followed Idlebird and Brown were Pinkey Hall and James T. Murphy. Private businesses and city employment were not sufficient to sustain both the white and African-American Workforce. Hence, one of the employment options left for many African-Americans was chopping and picking cotton in the Brazos River Bottom.

(Private)

In the Brazos River Bottom cotton crops were plentiful; African-Americans picked and pulled cotton. In some cases entire families, fathers, mothers and children picked. Mothers, mine included, carried their babies to the cotton field, as they could not afford to pay someone to keep their little ones. The babies were placed on the cotton sacks and dragged as mothers picked, and taken off at the weighing scale. It was alleged that Mr. Jackson and his family made enough money picking cotton to retire. Surely this was an exaggeration, but Mr. Jackson did boast openly of their weekly earnings.

Picking cotton was one of the most humiliating and back breaking jobs performed by African-Americans. They had to awake very early in order to catch a truck that hauled them to the cotton fields. The cotton truck haulers were primarily African-Americans and Mexican-Americans. The more popular haulers were William Benford, Tom Butler, Charlie Perry, Will Sanders and his son Collie. Rudy Gregoria was the more popular of the Mexican-American haulers. D.D. Catalina and Don Fazzino's brother were the two Italian-Americans who hauled cotton pickers to their farms. The work day was from sun up to sun down in the brutal Texas heat. Picking cotton was made even more miserable as crop dusters sprayed DDT that burned as it stuck to the skin.

Working in cotton fields was not preferable, but for many families it was the major source of income. Many, though not all, children were dependent upon the income from picking cotton to purchase school clothing and supplies. In general, kids and parents from every sector of Bryan picked cotton. A sample of the individuals (including me) and families who picked, are as follows: Willie Albert, Bass Butler, Lucas, Luke, Mollie, Hermon, "Sunny" Sanders, Nelsons, Wilsons, McCoys, Sterlings, Childs, Martins, Perrys, Henrys, Davenports, Turners, Allens, Wiliams and Smiths.

It was during the cotton days that I was introduced to watermelon rind preserves and wiener spaghetti by Anna McCoy, my neighbor. She reared four grandchildren, three boys and one girl, after their mother died early. Anna picked a little cotton and with meager means she found a way to feed her grandchildren. One of the clever ways she fed the children was wiener spaghetti. She would buy a box of spaghetti and tomato sauce or paste and make enough to feed four children and a neighbor or two. She would buy a watermelon, after eating the meat of the melon, she would use the rind to make preserves that would supplement the children's breakfast.

After cotton farmers, one of, if not the largest private single employer in Bryan, was the Allen Academy, formerly located on E.21st Street. The Academy provided employment for the following men, and their families: Wes Adams, Andrew Brown, Dolly Bisor, Willie Burton, Henry Dunn, Leroy Gator (who retired after fifty years), Rufus Graves, "Uncle" Mouton, Charlie Parnell, Tom Henry Rice, Jr., "Doc" Rogers, Leonard Rouse, "Sunny" Sanders, W.D. "Screwball," Archie Sims, Freddie Watson, "Buddy Williams, Freddie Williams, Ira Williams and me. Texas A and M University (Texas A and M College) was another source of employment for some African-Americans. For example, Charlie Mason was a "top cook" in the University Dining Hall and Memorial Student Center (MSC) Bowling Alley Cafeteria; Julia Shields worked in the University Dining Hall, William Smith and I set bowling pins in the MSC. Herman Brown and Robert Shields worked in the MSC before they enlisted in the US Navy; Leroy Gibbs worked in the MSC before he enlisted in the US Air Force. John Blackshear and other African-Americans worked at Texas A and M, but their names are unknown.

Chapter 4

African American Veterans (E.A. Kemp or Bryan)

In keeping with a tradition dating back as early as 1639 (Battle 2006, p.129.) African-Americans have served in the military, including WW-I, WW-II, Korea and Vietnam. But, this chapter will focus primarily on those who served in WW-II, Korea and Vietnam. Many (Negro) African-American sons and daughters left Bryan to serve in a war, in places they had never heard of and returned to the same segregated conditions they left. They fought, bled and died on the continents of Africa, Asia and Europe, only to come back home to unchanged educational, employment and housing conditions. However, their experiences exposed them to travels and seeing things in a different way. For example, some G.I.'s like Luther Bell, Clayburn Greer, James Johnson and Isaiah Martin moved to the West Coast and Pacific Northwest and never returned to Bryan. They found a better life in San Francisco, Portland and Seattle. Some, not all, names and pictures of the men and women who served in WW-II are listed in a book entitled: The Men and Women In WW-II From Brazos County and Aggie Veterans. However, below are the names of only African-American Veterans, most of who were, from Bryan and or attended E.A. Kemp Junior-Senior High School; their names are in alphabetical, from left to right, order below.

Billy Anderson	Joe A. Bernal	Raymond Bowser
Willie M. Bowser	Johnny Brown	Charlie Buchanan
Isaac Buchanan	James L. Buchanan	Benny Calhoun
Thomas Calhoun	Henry Carter	Roosevelt Clopton (O)
Benny Cunningham(PH)	Frank Ellis	Jonathan Gay

Isaiah Gooden
Steve Green
Arthur D. Hamilton
Lavaughn Hawkins
James Johnson
James Kennard
Fred Martin
W.Z. Nelson (PH)
Tommie L. Person
John H. Robertson
Willie Shaw, Jr.
Jester W. Smith
Willie Stephen
Tollie N. Thompson
Searcy Toliver
Burnise Williams
Emmett Walton

Lesley Green, Jr.
Toy Green (PH)
Edgar Hamilton
Albert Hayes
Nathaniel Johnson
Otis Laws
Ocil McGee
Sandford Nutall (PH)
Lamar Porter
William T. Ross
Daniel Smith, Jr.
L.C. Smith
Archie Suseberry, Sr.
Curley Thornton
Herbert Wallace
Woodrow Wilson

Rodney Green
Andrew Griffin
Arthur D. Hawkins
B.L. Johnson (K)
Obie Jones
William A. Laws
Andrew Mitchell
Ernest Payton
"Bubba" Rayford
Richard Shaw
James Smith
Woodrow W. Smith
Robert L. Thomas
Daniel O.Toliver
Rayfield L. Whitman
Randolph Wright, Jr.

An incomplete list of other WW-II Veterans, not mentioned above, including women who served during World War-II, are listed below.

Elijah Adams
Richard Childs
Samuel Ellis
Della Harris' brother(K)
Clancy Jones
Lawrence King
Isaiah Martin
Virgil Peterson
Johnny Robertson
James Thomas
Odis T. Walton, Sr.
Herman Williams
Milton Greer
Benney Leon Wilson
Savannah Smith Williams

Luther Bell
John Robert Clay
Clayburn Greer
Virgil T. Hickman
Needie Jones' Son
George Lewis
Url Ocheltree
Leon Pillows
Paul Scott
Ples Turner
Samuel B. White
Odessa Clopton
Marvin Walton
Anna Elmore

H.B. Buggs
Lonny Deere
Milton Gross
J.D. Hill
C.W. Kennard
Eugene Littleton (PH)
Alandrus Peterson, Sr.
Columbus Robinson
Clarence Sterling
Lawrence Wallace
"Sonny Man" White
Herman S.Williams
Joanna Hightower
Jessie M. Newsome

O-Officer, K-Killed, PH-Purple Heart

A special note is captured in the New York Amsterdam News, December 5, 1942, page 2, at Key Field, Mississippi: A Master Sergeant at the age of 23 in less than three months is a record established by Edgar L. Sadberry of Bryan, Texas. Edgar earned a Bachelor of Science in Agriculture from Prairie View College and was the brother of Oliver Wayne Sadberry, Principal of Washington Elementary School. The Sadberry brothers a total of seven, were all college graduates. According to the Bryan Daily Eagle from January 19, 1941 until September 21, 1945 over six hundred African-American men and women from Bryan and Brazos County volunteered or were drafted into the military. The majority of the men served in the US Army, and was from Bryan.

After the war, the government sponsored three vocational training sites for professional barbers, mechanics and tailors. African-American Veterans interested in becoming barbers attended the site located on the corner of 21st and N. Bryan Streets. Jettie Parks was the manager of the training site for barbers. Veterans interested in learning how to become tailors trained at the site located on W.19th and N. Bryan Streets. The manager for this site was John L. (Lev) Thomas. Veterans interested in mechanics trained at the site located on W.19th and San Jacinto Highway. H. K. Harnsberry was the supervisor for this site and Ernest Moore was one of the certified instructors. When the mechanics training was discontinued, the building was converted to the Three Aces Night Club.

As with WW-II, African-American citizens of Bryan served in 1950-53. Some of the young men were drafted their senior year; others volunteered. A few of the ones who were drafted returned after the conflict and received their diplomas. Some of the names, not all, of the sons and daughters of E.A. Kemp High who served during the Korean Conflict, are as follows: Betsy Brown, Claude A. Brown, Ernest Brown, Franklin Brown, Herman O. Brown, Fred Burton, Ralph Campbell, Freddie Carter, Ollie Carter, Vernon Chambers, Odessa Clopton, Sloan Clopton, Edward Colquitt, James Cooper, L.C. Davis, Wendell Davis, Joe Dupree, Curtis Duren, H.P. "Frock" Emanuel, Eugene Garvin, Leroy Gibbs, L.C. Gipson (killed), Stanley Griffin, Benny Gross, James Harnsberry (WO), James Harrison, Virgil T. Hickman, Lester Lee Holland, William Hughes, Woodrow Johnson, J.W. Jones, Roosevelt Littlejohn, Robert "Billy" Martin, Curtis Miles, M.L. Mitchell, Mavis Morgan, Sam Mosley, Jr., Eugene Nixon, Lawrence "Big Boy" Nutall, Felix Petty, Waldo Quarles, Homer Rice, Tom Henry Rice, Jr., Nettie Mae Richardson, James Eddie Rooks, Andrew"Buddy" Smith, Fred Douglas Smith, Joe Solomon, John Steen, Ray Steen, Willard Taylor, Archie Suseberry, Jr., Paul Toliver, R.C."Bucket"Wallace, Samuel Walker, James Arthur Walton, Paul Walton, James Aaron Ward, Hiwatha Webber,

Marion"Buck"Williams, Freddie Williams, Levi Williams, Dan Wilson, Hampton Taylor and Robert Wyatt.

Some of the same veterans who served in Korea also served in Vietnam; their names are included with the men who served in Vietnam, as follows: Jeff Bailey*, Arthur "Bo" Benford Claude A. Brown*, Herman O. Brown*, James Cooper*, Booker T. Davenport, Robert Dunn, Leon B. Gafford, Sid Garner, Howard Gibbs, Alvin Green (Purple Heart), Howard Green (Purple Heart), Maurice Green, Jr.,Virgus Green, Albert Griffin, Ocie Hall, Jr., James Harnsberry, (WO)*, Lou James Hines, Leon Houston (Purple Heart), Shedrack Houston, James Irvin, Donald Ray Johnson, Rastine "Foxall"Jones*, Robert McGhee, James E. Martin, Robert "Billy" Martin*, Curtis Miles*, Willie S. Mitchell, Willie Morrow (WO)*, Ernest Parker, John Parker, Shelton Parker, Curtis Perry, Bobby Phillips, Homer Rice*, Robert J. Shields*, Jesse Sanders, Clarence Simpson, James Simpson, Willie C. Smith, Elijah Thompson, Roger Turner, Elvin Walker, R.C. "Bucket" Wallace*, Alvin Walton, James Emmett Walton, Tollie Waller and George Riley Williams.

WO-Warrant Officer
*In service during Korean Conflict

Chapter 5

Small Business Owners (African-Americans and Italian-Americans)

Many African-Americans owned a variety of small businesses that provided them a level of independence, although they could not escape the tenets of segregation. Nonetheless, they were far better off than African-Americans who were fully dependent on white business owners for employment. As indicated between 1880-1910 black barbers, butchers and grocers provided services to the black community.(Brundige 1986, p.11) The total black commerce, which included merchants, craftsman and professions did not make up but about ten percent of the heads of black families.(Brundige 1986, p. 11) Apparently the rest of the population worked in menial jobs such as farmers, day laborers and domestics; see earlier section on employment opportunities.

African-American Businesses Downtown

Bryan was a divided city geographically with African-Americans occupying the North end of the city, and split between the Westside and Eastside. In downtown Bryan their small businesses were concentrated between 21st, 22nd and N. Bryan Streets. However, as you will see later there were a variety of businesses in the neighborhoods. Most of the downtown businesses consisted of professional barber shops and taxi cabs. For example, the following barbers were downtown: Hilbert Clopton, W. B. McQueen, Tommy Murphy, Jettie Parks, Jeremiah Smith and Searcy Toliver. Downtown Taxi Cab operators were: Henry Jenkins, Fred

Martin, Milas Moore, O.C. Parks and Alton Thomas. Henry Jenkins and Garfield Scott operated cafes, Ed Pigford and John L "Lev" Thomas had Real Estate Offices, John L. also operated a dry cleaners and tailor shop. Dr. Samuel Sealey's (MD) medical clinic was on the second floor of the building owned by Henry Jenkins. Clyde Gilmore owned a record shop next door. Dr. William A. Hammond, Sr., (MD) operated a medical clinic and office on the corner of 21st and N. Bryan Street. There were three beer taverns downtown, two between 20th and 21st Streets (operators unknown) and the third one on N. Bryan Street operated by Henry Haley. Ray Tarver owned a café on N. Bryan Street.

On the Eastside and Westside there were a number of small business owners. Starting on the Eastside, Mary Adams owned a laundry on Dansby Street that provided employment for Willie Freeman, Erie Lokelton, Vivian Peterson (my mother) and Parthenia Webber Smith. Rossetta Johnson owned a barbecue pit, café and beauty shop. The boy who lived with her, called "Sunny," James Johnson, helped in the café. If you made friends with him he would share some of the spoils. Julia Shields owned Bob's Confectionery, where delicious malts and hamburgers were made, and a few grocery items were stocked too. In addition, it had a jukebox; the malts, hamburgers and jukebox made the confectionery a very popular spot for young people on the Eastside and Westside to congregate. Her son Robert and daughter Minnie operated the business. Odis T. Walton Sr., owned the small Candy Hill Grocery Store before serving in WW-II. Not very long after he returned, he built a commodious store on the corner of Candy Hill and Pierce Streets. The store no-longer exist, but when it did it was well stocked with a:1) variety of meats, 2) dairy products, 3) dried goods, 4) canned goods, 5) notions, 6) produce, 7) hunting items, 8) tobacco products and 9) kerosene and gasoline. He also owned several apartments next to the store. Odis Walton was more than a grocery store owner, he was an entrepreneur. He owned another grocery type store on South Pierce Street about four blocks from his Candy Hill store. The store was sold later to Sam Restivo's

Pictured is one of several barbershops that was located in downtown Bryan between 21st and 22nd Streets and N. Bryan Street.

son and converted to a beer tavern and café. The tavern was operated by Sonny "Man;" the café by his parents. The tavern was frequented by adults who listened to Howlin Wolf, Muddy Waters and other "Gut Bucket" music. The café was where the young crowd congregated and treated themselves to a plate of smoked sausage and sweet potatoes, one of the specials. After Sonny Man and his parents, the tavern only was managed by Eddie B. Booker.

On East 19th Street (now MLK) Odis owned a Confectionery, Jean's Sewing Shop, with an apartment on the second floor and the OK Motel. Jean's Sewing Shop became a shoe repair shop operated by Roy King. After the shoe shop, it became a beauty shop operated by Pearlie Mae Murphy. The confectionery/café became a sub US Post Office and Polling Place. P.J. Stearne, referred to earlier, owned the grocery store, (previously owned by Lester Cunningham) on E.19th across the street from Odis' places. His store was stocked with a variety of meats, produce, dairy products, and was where students from Washington Elementary School could buy lunch. P.J. sold the store later to Don Fazzino where the practice of selling lunch to students continued. Guy and Bruce Barrow owned a grocery store on Henderson Street. Pete and Sonny Man White's mother operated a small café like store on East 21st Street where sodas and potato chips primarily were sold. But it was a fairly popular place because young people could dance to tunes on the juke box. African-Americans owned convenience stores on both Eastside and Westside before they were very popular. These stores were conveniently located in the immediate neighborhood and carried such items as bread, milk, snack foods, sodas and ice creams. There were four convenience stores on the Eastside; Tom Peterson and Clayburn Greer, Sr., located on the corner of Weaver and Pierce Streets. Emmett Walton located on the corner of Branch and Pierce Streets and William Groce's store was on Waco Street.

Johnny Robinson, a WW-II Veteran, and the first African-American Master Plumber, in Bryan owned a plumbing business on the Eastside and provided employment for J.C. Davis. Jordan Nelson owned a plumbing business on the Westside and provided employment for Will Smith. "Doc" Henderson and C.W. Kennard owned a concrete business and provided employment for John D. White who was in college and two of Mr. Henderson's sons.

There were three funeral homes in Bryan owned by African-Americans, Ed Scott's Funeral Home located on E.20th Street, Jones Mortuary located on E.19th Street and Daniel and Son's Funeral Home on W.20th Street. Jimmy Bell was Assistant Supervisor for Atlanta Life Insurance Company, Ernest H. Cass of Universal Life Insurance Company; S.P. Redden sold life insurance; W.C. Daniel, Sr. owned a funeral home and sold burial insurance. There were four day care/centers owned by African-Americans on the Eastside, Lula Dean, Minnie Bennie, Helen Simpson and Betty Suseberry Hanks. Lula Dean was located on the corner of E.20th and Houston Streets; Helen Simpson was located on Pierce Street; Minnie Bennie was located on E.19th Street and the corner of Highway 6 South, and Betty Suseberry is still located on the corner of Dansby and Bradley Streets.

Grocery and Convenience Stores
(Westside)

Sam Mosley's Grocery and Market located on W.19th Street was comparable to Odis Walton's Candy Hill Store in every way, plus he provided home delivery. He also owned facilities that John R. Clay rented for a shoe repair shop, a café/restaurant operated by Horace Nelson, and some rental property. Elmer and Lindsay Grays owned a modest grocery store located on San Jacinto Highway between 17th and 18th Streets. Rachel Cavitt owned a grocery store on W. 19th Street near San Jacinto Highway. Fred Evans was owner of a grocery store located on W. 28th Street. Clarence Johnson and Fred Martin operated a convenience store located on Florida Street; Jody Neal owned a convenience store near Doll's Beauty Shop on W.19th Street similar to the ones located on the Eastside (mentioned earlier). Robert Jones operated a place located between farW.17th and 18th Streets similar to Mrs. White's place on E.21st Street (referenced earlier).T.C. Calhoun owned Calhoun's Grocery located on West Muckleroy Street.

Barbeque Pit Owners-Operators
(Eastside)

Barbeque pits were another popular small business owned by African-Americans.There were a minimum of eight located on the Eastside. Henry Elarms on Pierce Street, Aaron Johnson on 20th Street and Rosetta Johnson (no relations) on Dansby Street, William "Rag" Mathis on Preston Street. Will Nettles on 18th Street, Four-Way Inn, Modern Club on 19th Street and Lester Nowlin Bronx Café on 18th Street specialized in barbeque. May Atkins was another barbeque pit owner.

Beauty Shops-School- Barber Shop
(Eastside)

African-American Beauty Shops were plentiful on the Eastside, starting with Nettie Richardson Clay's Beauty Shop on Preston and 21st Streets, Birdie Davis

Green's Shop (a graduate of Joyce and Cecil Wooley's Beauty School on Waco Street), Rosetta Johnson's Shop (mentioned earlier) on Dansby Street, Lelia Latson, Cassie Rice and Joyce Wooley had beauty shops on Pierce Street (Aslee Sims and Annette Idlebird Stephney) were operators; Joyce also had a barber shop on Pierce Street, Pearlie Murphy's Shop on E.19th Street; Gertie Randle and Cecil Wooley owned beauty shops on Henderson Street and Cecil's husband Joyce had a barber shop on Henderson Street too.

Barber and Beauty Shops
(Westside)

Eugene Garvin and Robert Newman owned barber shops on W.19th Street; Garvin's Shop was near George Washington Carver Elementary and Newman's was near Scanlin's Market. Alice Ellis had a barber shop on W.18TH Street, and Carrie Walker's Shop was on 28th Street. It is probably safe to assume African-American Women cared about their beauty and hair as evidenced by the number of beauty shops (salons). In addition to the shops located on the Eastside, Doll Sanders Mosley (Edna Neal, Ella Green and Nancy Murphy were operators) and Erie Knox owned beauty shops on W. 19th Street. Lillie Dunn and Lorraine White owned shops on or near Harlem Lane, and Beulah Young owned a shop on Lucky Street near San Jacinto Park. Jessie Rae Jefferson Nelson owned a beauty shop and café on San Jacinto Highway near the corner of W.17th Street. B-Neat Beauty Shop, Bessie O. Matthews proprietor, was located on W.17th and Columbus Streets.

Cafes-Diners-Snack Bars-Restaurants
(Westside)

Added to the cafes located downtown was Cavitt's Café on the corner of W. 21st and Sims Streets (which was later converted to a beer tavern). Scott's Diner located on W. 20th Street was owned by Garfield and Jessie Scott. Littleton's Snack Bar, owned by Earl and Alma Littleton; Nelson's Café owned by Horace Nelson were both on W.19th Street. Richard Childs and Jessie Rae Jefferson owned cafes on the corners of San Jacinto Highway and W. 17th Street. Lizzie Green owned a café on W. 22nd Street and Phillip's Café and Barbeque was located on Saunders Street. Scott's Diner was the eatery for out of town athletic teams that competed against E.A. Kemp High School. It was also one of the places Kemp faculty and students could buy hot lunches (as mentioned earlier).

Pictured is what was Cavitt's Cafe located on W. 21st Street.

Littleton's Snack Bar provided lunch too, but mostly to students. Mr. Littleton's son James and daughter Faye worked the lunch hour during school. She was generous; when some students (including me) could not pay full price for lunch, she accepted what they could pay. Later, when in the Navy, I attempted to show my appreciation by sending magazines and other small gifts when she was attending college. Littleton's was more than fast food; it was a place where benches were provided for young people to congregate after school and weekends. The snack bar was also a place of employment for students like Adolph Johnson, Jr., Robert Richardson, Jr., Dewayne Mosley and me (briefly) while waiting to attend college. Bessie Shannon owned a barbeque-café that was originally located on W. 19th Street near San Jacinto Highway. The place was relocated to Peale Street and is currently under the management of her daughter as a café only. Rosie's Barbeque was located on W. 19th Street and Charlie McNeil's Barbeque was located on W.16th and Hall Streets. In addition to his barber shop, Eugene Garvin owned a snack bar.

Body Shops-Garages-Scrap Metal-Junk Yards-Service Stations (Eastside and Westside)

Nick Benford owned a scrap metal (junk yard) located on the corner of Dale and Candy Hill Streets. Henry Clay owned a scrap metal (junk yard) on the corner of Henderson Street and Military Drive. Charlie Perry (popularly known as Charlie) owned a scrap metal (junk yard) on Houston Street in Freedmen Town.

Henry Carter operated a body shop and garage on the corner of San Jacinto Highway and W.17th Street; Steamer Johnson's Garage was located about three blocks North on San Jacinto from Henry Carter. Elmer and Lindsay Grays owned a large garage about two blocks South on San Jacinto Highway. Earnest Walker and James Taylor owned service stations, Taylor's Service Station had a garage attached. Both were located on W. 19th and San Jacinto Highway. Earnest Walker also owned a Gulf Service Station on San Jacinto and Jenkins Street; Milton Turner may have been the only African-American Body and Paint Shop in Bryan. Rastine Calhoun operated a scrap metal (junk yard) on Saunders Street near San Jacinto Park; Isaac Madison also operated a scrap metal(junk yard). Tom Thornton owned a garage on W.19th Street near N. Bryan Street.

In addition to the businesses mentioned above, African-Americans owned dry cleaners, hotels, laundries, radio/television and shoe repair shops in downtown Bryan and on both sides of the city. Rastine Jones operated a dry cleaners downtown on N. Bryan Street. Chester Adams owned O K Cleaners and Laundry on the corner of E.18th and Highway 6 South near Williams' Hotel. The largest (modern) dry cleaners and laundry was owned by Dr. William A. Hammond, Sr. It was a modern plant that included pickup and delivery service located on W.17th Street. James Hedge was proprietor of the West End Cleaners located on W.19th Street across San Jacinto Highway. Vern Mayo and Rachel Cavitt owned a Cleaners on W. 19th Street too. John Robert Clay had the distinction of owning-operating two shoe repair shops, one between E.21st and Preston Streets and the number two shop on W.19th Street. Roy King operated his shop on E.19th Street and Aaron Butts' shop was on the Westside near Lucky Street. Roosevelt Lucky owned a television shop on Saunders Street and Lewis Rice owned a radio repair shop on the Westside. Dr. William A. Hammond, Sr. operated a kindergarten facility near the hospital. Rosetta Cheeks owned a day care center on Columbus and W.18th Streets. Mr. and Mrs. J.W. Bell owned the Ding Dong Bell Kindergarten and Nursery on W.17th Street. Felix Jones may have been the only African-American in Bryan who owned a house relocating (moving) business concern. Dossie Foster was owner of another O.K. Cleaners which was located on N. College Avenue.

Night Clubs-Beer (Joints) Taverns (Eastside-Westside)

Other small businesses owned-operated by African-Americans in Bryan were places to buy, drink beer and for the over twenty crowd to socialize. Some night clubs were referred to as "beer joints" because they did not qualify as night clubs based on on the opinions of the community. Such establishments were located on both sides of the city, starting with the Cotton Club located on the Eastside just off of Waco Street was owned by "Fatty" Robb. It was a very popular spot in the late forties and mid fifties and was revived intermittingly during the late fifties. The Four-Way Inn located on E.18th Street near Highway 6 South was known as a "honky tonk." It had a reputation for catering to a rough clientele where a number of citizens met their demise, including Daniel Morgan. Of the three beer joints downtown, Henry Haley operated the one on N. Bryan (mentioned earlier) that attracted a rowdy crowd. Owners-operators of the other two are unknown. The Night Spot, another beer joint, was located on E. Tabor Street and was known for being a dangerous place. In fact citizens known to me were mortally wounded in this establishment. The Tin Shack located at 17th Street and Highway 6 was another beer joint that attracted a rowdy crowd. The Hole in the Wall operated by Hazel Coleman was located on Pierce Street near the E. 19th attracted a variety of clients. On the corner of Washington Street and Highway 6 was another unsavory beer joint. Charlie Perry operated a beer joint in Freedmen Town near Highway 6 and E.18th Street and the Big Apple Night Club on W.19th Street and San Jacinto Highway. Richard Childs operated a popular night club on the corner of W.17th Street and San Jacinto Highway that is now a Sea Food Store. On 17th Street and down from Richard's Place, "Buddy" Caldwell operated a night spot. A block from Buddy's" was the Tick Tock Club operated by Zellie Newton. Harmon "Sun" Bell operated the Blue Moon Club located off San Jacinto-Highway 21 extended. The Merry-Maker was on W. Highway 21 beyond the Blue Moon. Ennis Green operated a beer joint and rooming house on Hall Street and McGee's Hotel was on San Jacinto Highway. Lizzie Horn operated a rooming house on the Westside on or near California Street.

Italian-Americans: Small Business Owners

According to sources by (Rosemary Boykin1996, n.p.) and (Handbook of Texas Online n.p.) early Italian Immigrants came to Texas through New Orleans, Louisiana; most of them were Sicilians. They settled in the Brazos River Valley and learned cotton farming; however many of their children and grandchildren left cotton farms and moved to Bryan and became businessmen. Some of them could have been the children and grandchildren who lived and owned businesses in African-American neighborhoods (mentioned earlier). For exam-

Italian-American Nick Dielo Grocery Store and Beer Joint located on E. 19th and N. Polk Streets.

ple, the following Italian-Americans lived and or owned businesses in African-American communities: Don Fazzino owned a grocery store on E.19th Street that he bought from P.J. Stearne. He also owned the Harlem Drive Inn located between W.20th and 21st Streets and the Modern Club on E. 19th Street; both attracted a more sophiscated clientele. Jake Cangelosi, Nick Dielo, Tony Boe Kelley and M. Ruffino owned grocery stores on the Eastside. Nick also owned a beer joint on E. 19th that attracted an older and less urbane crowd. Tony owned a Beer Tavern on Pierce and Bradley Streets and attracted a demographic much like Nick Dielo. Jake Cangelosi owned a grocery store near Washington and Apple Streets and Highway 6 North. While Charles Fererri did not live in the neighborhood but he owned the Sugar N Spice Drive Inn located on Highway 6 North near Washington Street. Sam Restivo owned a grocery store on E.19th Street, and one of his sons (mentioned earlier) bought Odis Walton's Store on South Pierce Street and converted it to a beer joint and café. Luke Graffizi, Sam Lampo, Charles Ruffino, and Frank Scanlin were grocery store owners who lived in Westside neighborhoods. In African-American neighborhoods where Italian-Americans lived and owned businesses they provided employment for members of the immediate community. For example, Jack

Johnson, Arthur Dunn and Anne King worked in the grocery store or other capacity for Don Fazzino.Vernice Turner and Ruby Davenport worked at the Harlem Drive Inn, Joyce Thomas, et al, worked at the Modern Club owned by Don Fazzino. James Banks, James McCoy, James Martin, Charles Sterling, Leroy Sterling, and Bunny Wright were employed by Charles Fererri. Tony Boe Kelley employed Mrs. Rosetta (last name not known), Tommy Traylor, Frank Perry and Rudolph Johnson were employed by Frank Scanlin.

Chapter 6

"Shot Gun" Rent Houses and Government Projects

Poor and limited employment opportunities for African-Americans translated into the inability to pay school taxes and purchase homes. This increased the demand for rental housing. Both African-Americans and whites owned and rented substandard three room houses referred to as "shot gun houses" because you could see through them without obstructions. Most of the houses, but not all, were unpainted, without running water, indoor plumbing, wallpaper and window treatment. Even though the houses were substandard, they kept families (mine included) from living on the streets or being homeless. My family was able to purchase a lot and build a little house on the corner of Branch and Pierce Streets eliminating their dependency on such housing. But not before we had lived in two different shot gun houses on Henderson and Dansby Streets located on the Eastside of Bryan.

Starting on Dale Street Elliott Myers, Sr. owned two or three rent houses; one was occupied by Ida Davis, Johnny, Mickey, Jean and Sunny. The second house was occupied by Lillie Mae Brisby, Cleveland, Frank and two sisters. When Ida Davis vacated the house, one of the Mitchell sisters assumed residency. Two additional families, the Blues and Thurmans, occupied the house previously occupied by the Brisby family. Further South on Dale Street near Middle Street Joyce Wooley's brother and his family lived in one of three shot gun houses, Charlie Crawford, his wife, and her daughter lived on the same block. Dyke Hicks, his wife, Bobby and his sister lived in the last house on Dale Street near Candy Hill Street. On the corner of Candy Hill and Dale Streets were several houses that were occupied by the Colemans, Thompsons, Blues, and the Mitchell family. Further South on Dale and the corner of Bradley Street lived Lee Doris Jones and her daughter. On Bradley Street directly behind Lee Doris lived a Mr. Watson in a house that is still standing. Continuing on Dale Street to Military Drive were four more unpainted houses. Two were occupied by individuals whose names have been forgotten. The third house was occupied by the Gator family and the fourth by Roxanne and her sister.

"Shot Gun House" On Dale and Bradley Streets

East of Dale on Pierce Street were three rent houses where bachelors Cornelius Kilpatrick, Harris, and Gibson lived. Gibson owned a mule and hired out to plow gardens and Harris had been married to Della Lewis. Directly behind Kilpatrick on Candy Hill Street lived C.L. Smith (known as C.L.). Continuing South on Pierce Street past Bradley Street were four or five more shot gun houses. The first house was occupied by a woman known as "Sweet Momma" and her two sons; next door lived Clarence Ross and Bertha. Next to them lived Ira Williams, his wife and two sons. In the fourth house lived Emmadine and her family. In the back of these families was a cluster of the same type houses, one of which was occupied by a man called "A.J." and his family. I believe James Otis Henry's relatives lived in the next house, and at one time Freddie, Dorothy and their daughter also lived in the same cluster. Approximately two blocks further on Pierce and the corner of E.19th Street was a group of houses where relatives of Aubrey Hill lived. Turning the corner onto E.19th were three houses: two were occupied by the Nixon family, Sunny Caldwell's sister and son. Making a U-Turn on Pierce and where Henderson Street terminates, is Waco Street. People who lived on this street were quite proud of their community, but some of them were subjected to the same poor housing conditions, too.

1950 "Shot Gun House" MLK-Pierce St.

Starting on North Henderson Street, near Pierce Street extended, now MLK, Arthur Brown, his mother, sister and her family occupied two separate rent houses.

On the opposite side of the street Rose Loud and her two sons lived in a rent house owned by Rose Castle. Willie Mae Adams and daughters lived in the same block. Roland Hunter and his mother lived three doors from Willie Mae, next to Juanita Mundine Nix. Two blocks from Roland were three houses, owned by El-

1950 "Shot Gun House" on Bradley between Dansby and 21st Streets still occupied

liott Myers and an individual named Ware. Two of the houses were occupied by two families by the name of Sterling and Phillips; my family occupied the third house. Mary Adams owned one unpainted shot gun house across the street that was occupied by two different Smith families. Eddie Smith, Sr. and his family were the first occupants; Gladys and her family were the second occupants. At the end of Henderson Street and Military Drive the corner house was occupied by a man whose nickname was "Chummy" who died in a fire. Across the street from "Chummy" lived a Korean Conflict Veteran and his wife. In the same block going West were three more houses; "Skeeter" and his mother lived in one, the Henrys lived next door, but the third family was not known. As of October 2009 the Henry's house is still there and occupied by a new owner. During a recent trip to the old neighborhoods I noticed that three shot gun houses are still standing to remind African-Americans of an unpleasant housing experience.

Beginning in the first block of N. 21st Street (near the original New Zion Baptist Church) there were two shot gun rent houses. One was occupied by Doris and her brother Israel. The occupants of the second house were unknown. Moving South on 21st Street to where it intersects with Dansby Street Pearl Forward owned several of the same type houses, but hers were painted. As I recall, Christine, her daughter Jo Ann and son Dan occupied the one next to the Fennells. My mother, sister, and I lived across the street from Christine and the Baileys and Dorseys lived next door. James Otis Henry and his father lived in the last house on the first block near the corner of Dansby and Candy Hill Streets. At the end of Dansby on Military Drive were three more houses; the first house was occupied by Johnny Floyd and his parents. The second house was occupied by his grandparents and occupants of the third house were not known.

Going West on Military was Freedmen Town, an addition with a large concentration of shot gun houses. Families living in Freedmen Town experienced similar if not the same poor housing conditions. Near Shiloh Baptist Church on the side of Houston Street where Earnest and Corrine Cass lived were three or four shot gun houses. Joe Turner occupied one house, the Perrys lived in a second house, and a third house was occupied by another Turner family. At E.18th and Houston Streets, Emmett Matthews lived on the corner. Going North on Houston Street about a block were more houses occupied by another family of Perrys, Browns, Lenora, Leroy, "Brother" Minnie, Howard and his wife. Crossing Highway 6 South and 17th Street Pauline and her family lived.

The street where the author lived.

Traveling from the Eastside to the Westside of Bryan many of the same kind of rent houses were seen throughout the neighborhoods. Housing conditions on the Eastside were replicated on the Westside of Bryan. The one significant exception were the ones owned by Dr. William A. Hammond, Sr. which were painted his signature colors of white with green trim. Starting from Boulevard Street near Highway 6 North and San Jacinto Highway to 22nd Street, up and down main streets were rent houses occupied by low income families. The same was true for cross streets, including Sims, Logan, Sterling, Randolph, Congress, Hall, Hudson, Dean, Harlem Lane, Florida, Murkleroy and streets in between.

(Westside Government Projects)

However, in the 1950's government projects were constructed on a site adjacent to Carver Elementary School. This may have marked the first time many families had running water, paved streets and semi-central heating and air conditioning. For many including my mother, two sisters and I, living in the projects was a huge step up. However, getting a rental unit was not so easy because the demand for housing exceeded availability. Therefore, it was important and often necessary for applicants to have someone of influence speak in their behalf. Applicants who worked for the city of Bryan or well-to-do white families were often granted units before individuals who did not have the same privileges. The demand for decent housing was so extremely great until a second phase of government projects were built opposite the site near Carver Elementary School on W.19th Street.

(Eastside Government Projects)

Since an identical need for decent housing existed on the Eastside, construction was begun on government projects on the Eastside shortly after the second phase was completed on W.19th. These projects were constructed on E. 21st Street, at the end of Dansby, Military Drive and Henderson Street. Again, the projects provided decent housing for many families, who, for the first time

A typical housing unit in the government projects on the Eastside.

lived on paved streets, had running water and semi-central heating and air conditioning. Over fifty years have passed, and the projects are still meeting the needs of families who had only known life in three room, see through houses. The projects provided decent affordable housing compared to the unpainted "shacks" that some could only afford. Rent payment in the projects was based on an individual's ability to pay, but each family enjoyed the same amenities. On a recent trip to the neighborhood near the Eastside Projects, I noticed only three shot gun houses are still standing to remind all of the stark contrast between housing conditions for African-Americans then and now.

Chapter 7

Hospitals and Medical Care

Historically African-American citizens of Bryan had medical doctors but not hospitals that were friendly and welcoming. The Bryan Hospital opened in 1913 and was operated by Dr. W.H. Oliver until 1933.(Anderson 2001, p. 32) The original building was a three story with 25 beds and located near downtown. The hospital closed after his death and reopened in 1934 under the management of Dr. R.B. Erlinger and Dr. R.B. Grant but was leased to the Sisters of St. Francis. The Sisters purchased the building in 1936 and renamed the facility St. Joseph. (St. Joseph Health System, n.p.) Today it is the St. Joseph Regional Medical Center. Dr. H.L. Fountain opened the Fountain Sanitarium in 1908 and Dr. Albert L. Mondrick developed a hospital in association with his practice in 1913. (Anderson 2001, p.32) In later years Bryan ISD named the Hammond-Oliver Health Sciences School in honor of Dr. William A. Hammond, Sr. and Dr. W.H. Oliver. All efforts to open and develop hospitals were private and there was not a general hospital in Bryan. Understanding again that Bryan was immutably segregated Dr.William A. Hammond, Sr., built a clinic in 1916 where African-Americans could readily receive professional consultation and medical attention or service. During this time there was one other African-

Dr. W. M. Hammond was one of few black surgeons Brazos County has ever had. He studied at Prairie A&M and later attended medical school. Dr. Hammond moved to Bryan from his hometown, Hammond, which was named after his family.

American physician, A.E. Thompson in Bryan, who also served as coach for the Bryan Public School for Colored football team. Prior to the clinic African-Americans were not readily able to get professional and medical services primarily because of either skin color or an inhospitable reception. Perhaps in some cases they were not served due to their inability to pay. As a result, many minor and more serious ailments were treated with home made remedies. For example, kerosene mixed with sugar was used to treat the common cold; kerosene was also used to treat a rusty nail stick, instead of a tetanus shot. Castor oil was another common remedy for colds along with eating Vic's Salve and being rubbed with a product called Penetro. Baking soda and Epson Salt were also common pharmaceuticals used to treat a variety of illnesses. Baking soda was also used as a dental prophylactic and for hygiene. Sardines, it was thought, would cure mumps when rubbed on the earlobes. More serious illnesses, medical needs or emergencies such as obstetrics were addressed by one of three known midwives, Ella Latson, "Old Lady" Calhoun (as she was known) and Minnie Thornton (known as Aunt Minnie). She was the aunt of Clifton and James (Jim) Greer; she delivered both of them and many others."Old Lady" Calhoun lived on the Eastside and when mothers were about to deliver their babies, it was common to hear someone say " better send for Old Lady Calhoun." This was during the time when doctors made home visits. After the baby was born, they would come and examine both the mother and baby.

Dr. Samuel J. Sealey was one of several Black Medical doctors in Bryan during the 1940s and 50s. He was respected in the community. His office was located on Main St. between 20th and 21st Streets.

In 1928 Brazos County employed an African-American Nurse to serve "Blacks." She also trained midwives at a Negro Health Center located on the campus of the Bryan Public School for Colored. (Eagle, May 6, 1929, p. 4) Dr. William A. Hammond, Sr. must have realized the clinic was not adequate for handling serious medical needs. So in 1929 he opened the sixteen bed Hammond Memorial Hospital on Randolph and W.17th Street, "Dedicated to Suffering Humans," that remained open into the 1950's. (Brundige 1986, p.106) Drs. Hammond, Sr., and Thompson were joined later by two other physicians, Drs. Samuel J. Sealy and J.M. Franklin. Dr. Sealy practiced medicine in Bryan and Madisonville until he and his family moved to Saint Louis, Missouri in 1950. Sarah Reed owned a Convalescent Home that was primarily for pregnant mothers but also served other ill patients. It was located on W. 19th Street not very far from Hammond's Hospital and was an important partner in the medical services offered to African-Americans. In addition to being a surgeon, owning clinic and hospital, he was an entrepreneur. He owned rent houses (stated earlier) that provided housing for low income families, a lumber yard and a kindergarten. He owned a laundry and dry cleaners that offered pickup and delivery service, which, as did his other enterprises, provided employment to a number of families. Dr. Hammond purchased land for the Grandview Cemetery for African-Americans. Added to his contributions above was involvement in civic issues, such as the Negro Chamber of Commerce and PTA.

In spite of a full schedule of civic and professional functions, Dr. and Mrs.William Hammond, Sr. were successful parents. They had seven children, six of whom lived. Four daughters and two sons all became professionals. Of the four daughters, Carolyn, who I met by phone while doing this project, became a physician, and is still active. Gladys became an educator, Prudence became an educator and a successful business woman. Lovie Jewell became a lawyer, returned to Bryan, where she may have been the second African-American to practice law. (McKay, Paul 1986, Black History) The older son, William Hammond, Jr. became a physician and the second son, Charles Hammond became a dentist. Carolyn lives in Laurel, Maryland, Gladys (it is believed) lived in Oklahoma where she taught school but may have moved to Ohio later, where Prudence may live or lived. Lovie Jewell lived in Bryan, as mentioned earlier. William A. Hammond, Jr. practiced medicine in California where some of his patients (who moved from Bryan to California) were former patients of his father. Charles Hammond lived and practiced dentistry in San Diego, California. There were three professional dentists who provided dental care to African-Americans, Drs. J.T. Canady, I. A. Carter and C.W. Flint. Dr. Carter took care of E.A. Kemp High School athletes when they received injuries in athletic events that required dental care or surgery. I knew Dr. Carter personally and his wife, Mrs. Irma Carter taught Social Studies at Washington Elementary School.

Chapter 8

Recreational Activities and Facilities

After school recreation was limited for both boys and girls as there was not a boys and girls club. Although it is reported that a YMCA was organized or proposed earlier in the century. (Brazos County Historical Time Line 1913, n.p.) As with most things educational and social, some African-American teachers made attempts to provide wholesome opportunities where boys and girls could interact socially, in friendly and safe environments after school. Oscar Pierce, Sr., father of Otis and Oscar Pierce, a civic and community minded parent, established the YAC Club for boys. Many young boys between the ages of twelve and eighteen participated in the YAC Club. There were some evening activities during the week but weekends they filled the days playing sports. Softball and baseball teams, for competition, were formed and sportsmanship and teamwork were constant themes of club members. Claude L. Scurry, the head coach of everything at E.A. Kemp Junior-Senior High School organized other recreational activities, such as boxing and scouting, as means of developing character and socialization skills. Most, but not all participated in the Boy Scouts because some parents could not afford the fees. However, the few who did participate, Claude Brown, Herman Brown, James H. Crawford, Charles Murphy, and Robert Shields, for example, said they enjoyed the canoeing and other activities. The younger boys, the ones who could afford it had an opportunity to join the Cub Scouts. Again, the boys who were members, for example Andrew Byrd, Jr.; Elliott Myers, Jr. and Weldon Walton all said they enjoyed themselves. Ennis Owens and David Parker exposed young boys to opportunities to develop character, team concepts and skills. They, too, were instrumental in creating a climate for competition in a formal supervised context through sports. Lula Dean, a day care owner mentioned earlier, provided Friday and Saturday, an opportunity for boys and girls to socialize in a formal setting. She allowed them to play a host of games; listen to music and demonstrate musical talent by playing the piano. Furthermore, she insisted they demonstrated acceptable social habits and respect for one another.

Pictured are the Teenkings at E. A. Kemp Auditorium. Left to Right: Dewayne Mosley, Nat Dove, Clinton Walton, Melvin Littleton and Rufus Green

Prudence Hammon Coker, one of Dr. Hammond's daughters demonstrated an interest in young girls, and provided an opportunity for them to learn proper etiquette, and other acceptable social graces. Bryan then, unlike later, did not have a Girl's Inc. or YWCA for young African-American females. However, there was a Recreational and Civic Club for female youth of Bryan; which became the Youth Center Club House. (B. C.H.S. 1885-1985, p. 2) In later years the Youth Center Club House was changed to its present name, the Bethune Woman's Club. (B.C.H.S., p.2) The Club has provided opportunities and sponsored a variety of activities for young girls; ladies and women. It is reported in Brazos County History: Rich Past-Bright Future that Arthur Keats, a teacher, saw the need for teenage recreation and opened a place and called it Keats' Hall and sponsored various activities.(Banks 1986, p.110) Collie Sanders, a Kemp student tried to provide a place for teenage recreation that was located on 28th Street, now Suncrest. There were other places that provided recreational opportunities for young people to congregate, and socialize after school, and weekends.

In addition to the ones mentioned above, such as Bob's Confectionery Walton's Confectionery, Robert Jones and a building next to the Tick Tock Night Club were intended for youth activities. But of all the places for teenage recreation KNOX's located on W.19th Street was the most popular. It was owned by Mr. Edward H. Knox, a former principal of Washington Elementary school but managed by Searcy Toliver, a WW-II Veteran. Youth from Bryan as well as the surrounding areas came to Knox's Place to dance to live and juke box music. One of the genuinely delightful and enjoyable times was after the Friday night athletic events when students would dance to the music played by Kemp High student musicians. Kemp always had talented young musicians, many of whom were tutored first by Mr. Hardy Murphy, Band Director until 1951 and later by Dr. Waymon Webster who was also a superb musician. Some of the musicians were Lorenzo "Bunny" Scurry who played in Las Vegas after leaving high school, Fred G. Smith who played with Ray Charles, arranged for Smokey Robinson, and earned a degree in music from Prairie View A and M University, and studied at the University of North Texas (UNT) formerly North Texas State University, and Sidney Earl Simpson. Another exceptional musician was Marion Jones, who was accepted in one of the jazz lab bands at the University of North Texas while still in high school, am told. Donald (Dickie) Childs and James Herman Alberson also attended UNT, and Horace Nelson who studied music at Prairie View A and M University. Ennis Green, Charles Watson, Clyde Dove, Albert Griffin, Willie C. Smith and Nathaniel Dove were all student musicians. Nathaniel has traveled internationally, playing in Tokyo and Paris, and was living in Bakersfield, California as of 2008. There were other talented musicians not mentioned above, such as Johnny Cunningham, Billy Ray Smith, Oliver Wayne Sadberry, Jr., "Billy"Walker, Fred Burton and Oscar Morgan, who moved to Dallas after school and I believe still lives there. All the efforts to provide recreational opportunities for young African-Americans were based on individual and or group initiatives. One group of individuals formed a gospel singing quartet and became the Utility Gospel Singers led by Jesse Lee Davenport; and used to broadcast on KORA AM Station in Bryan. Members of the Gospel Utility Singers included Anise Bell (tenor), Tom Butler, Marvin Cooper (baritone), Zelt Mims, Fred Smith, Charles Sterling (tenor and baritone and one of the lead singers), John L. Williams and Arthur Woodard. They were the inspiration for a young group of individuals who used singing as a recreational activity and would go from house to house singing. Even more, the recreational singing gave birth to a group called the Teenkings a Doo Wop singing group that consisted of Nat Dove, Rufus Green, Melvin Littleton, Dewayne Mosley and Clinton Walton.

Bryan, in the early years was segregated which meant public facilities were separated. As many of you know and have read, there were black businesses, schools for blacks and no intellectual means of expression. On January 18, 1906 it was reported in the Bryan Daily Eagle:

> The old Presbyterian Church has been purchased by C.G. Parsons and is being moved to the westside of town, corner of Clay and Wheelock streets where it will be used as a hall for colored society.(Eagle, n.p.)

On March 10, 1939, the Eagle reported:

> Feeling that the increasing Negro population is demanding wholesome places of leisure and that a substitute must be offered for places of amusement that often lead to crime. the Negro people have organized to make an effort to have a public library for them here. This Colored Library Association is presenting the Prairie View Dramatic Club in a three-act psychological thriller,'The Hat Mystery,' on Wednesday evening at 8:15 in the Kemp high school auditorium.(Eagle, n.p.).

As reported in Historic Brazos County by Robert Borden, Dr. I.A. Carter, African-American dentist, was elected chairman and H.K. Harnesberry as co-chairman. **NOTE: (in this book the name Harnesberry is also spelled Harnsberry)**

Other officers included Ellis Johnson, vice-chairman; Mrs. C.E. Cass, secretary; Imogene Sharp, corresponding secretary; I.L.Williams treasurer; and Reverend T.L. Sanders, chaplain. City librarian Miss. Margaret Sims addressed the third "mass meeting" of the association on March 19, 1939. Again, the Eagle reported on this meeting:

> Many white citizens also attended, among them being James A. Astin, Bryans's new city manager, who made an interesting talk on 'Delinquency Reduction Among Colored People.' He pointed out that a public library would be an important movement for such a reduction. In his brief address, he also commended the Boy Scout movement among the Negro people, and recommended Girl Scouts, which yet are to be organized.(Eagle, n.p.).

The Carnegie Library built with funds donated by Andrew Carnegie much later opened its doors to all citizens of the community.

A review of the literature on Bryan's Parks and Recreation revealed much. For example the city of Bryan did not give serious consideration to organized recreation for citizens until the 1920's. In 1920 city planners purchased 9.5 acres of land for the Sue Haswell Park and in 1957 a pool with a bath house was incorporated into the park structure. (A History of Bryan Parks and Recreation 1868-2004, p.2) Apparently, (more a guess) prior to this time Bryan did not have a city operated swimming pool. However, African-American citizens could only watch the white citizens swim in the pool. African-American boys swam in the American Legion tank located on Old Kurten Road and Waco Street. The tank also served as the baptismal for the original New Zion Baptist Church. James Allen Graves who lived on Old Reliance Road, Pierce Street extended, had a mud hole deep enough for swimming. Boys who had transportation to the Bryan Air Force Base that was located miles from the city could swim in the integrated pool. Finally, Allen Academy had a pool near its lake on the property where Henry Williams and his family lived. Although the pool was like a mud hole, except it had pool depth designations, we would trespass and swim during the week, weekends, and sometimes at night. African-Americans had to wait, until about 1957, for their own city operated swimming pool.

In 1946 the city purchased the "Poor Farm" which later became the Eastside Addition Park. (Bryan Parks, p.7) In 1956 a Bryan Daily Eagle Headline read as follows: "opening programs at Crockett, Bowie and Ben Milam Elementary Schools for whites and at Washington Elementary and E.A. Kemp Junior-Senior High Schools for black children." (Eagle 1956 n.p.) In 1957 the city purchased 23 additional lots that were added to the Poor Farm which had become the Eastside Addition Park. It was at this time that the first modern swimming pool for African-Americans was opened. At the same time a softball, tennis, soccer field, two pavilions, ten picnic tables and restrooms were added. (Bryan Parks, pp. 7, 21) In 1959 the Eastside Addition Park located on Martin Luther King and Moss Streets was renamed Sadie E. Thomas Memorial Park in honor of her contributions to education and recreation. (Bryan Parks, p.9) In 1971 Washington Park (on the former site of Washington Elementary School) was developed at the time with a basketball court and restrooms. Play ground equipment and improved lighting were added later. The oldest park in Bryan, Groves Addition Park, located between Wellington Street and the Southern Railroad was renamed Claude Scurry. (Bryan Parks, p5) Williams Park, located on the corner of W. Randolph and 21st Streets, site of the first disposal plant, was renamed Neal Park (1996) in honor of Robert C. Neal. (Bryan Parks, p.21) Bryan now has three parks named in honor of African-Americans. In 1998 the first Recreational Center was built adjacent to Neal Elementary School. (Bryan Parks, p.22)

The Queen Movie Theater in downtown, one of three segregated theaters.

There were four movie theaters in downtown Bryan, the Dixie, Palace, Queen and Starlite. The first three were owned by the Schulmans and were located on Main Street in downtown Bryan. The Starlite Theater owner was unknown but it was located on the North end of Bryan where the downtown African-American businesses were concentrated. Of the three theaters located on Main Street, African-Americans were permitted to attend the Palace but were limited to balcony seating. Even with restricted seating some of us made it a tribal ritual to attend the midnight shows every Friday night. Seating in the Starlite was unrestricted and the house was packed every Saturday with boys, mostly, who reveled in movies with Buster Crab, Tom Mix, Randolph Scott and Johnny Weissmuller (Tarzan). It was in the Starlite Theater where the movie "Look Out Sister" played, with Louis Jordan and Bob Scott whose brother Kermit Scott was on the 1930 Bryan Public School for Colored football squad. During that time the cost to see a movie was twenty-five cents and one could see the movie repeatedly. Another theater that was perhaps unknown to many citizens, was an outdoor sort of makeshift theater located on Pierce Street behind the "Beer Joint" owned by one of Sam Restivo's sons. Since it was outdoors it was hard to enjoy the movie while fighting off the mosquitoes.

Chapter 9

Newspaper and Information Sources

It, the Bryan Daily Eagle was the primary newspaper for citizens of Bryan, Texas for years. The paper, to my knowledge, was not hospitable in its coverage of African-American Citizens in its inception. For the most part, it reported unflattering stories about murders and vandalism; such information demeaned and maligned citizens of color. Eventually the Eagle's coverage changed and was slanted in a more positive direction. However, in the meantime if African-Americans wanted news and other information they had to import it from outside of Bryan. Two newspapers that carried stories with positive images and information about African-Americans were the *Chicago Defender* and *Pittsburg Courier.* James T. Murphy (referred to as J.T.) was the contact and distributor for the *Chicago Defender* and I was the local contact for the *Pittsburg Courier.* We received and delivered these papers to our respective customers. J.T. had a fairly large customer base which he successfully maintained for several years including while in high school. My customer base was quite small and not maintained very long. As I recall, an adult named Otis Johnson, who lived in Freedmen Town, was the contact and distributor for another imported paper, the name of which has been forgotten. Fred Hickman's father was the distributor of the Bryan Daily Eagle to the African-American community.

For a period of time Reverend C.C. Jammer, pastor of Lee Chapel Methodist Church, published the TREND Magazine. Perhaps it was intended to fill gaps left by the Eagle. The TREND provided local news about communities in Bryan and Brazos County. My first awareness of the magazine were two articles, one about Billy Ray Smith, who at the time was a student at Lincoln University in Pennsylvania. The second article was about my 1959 tour of Navy duty in Hawaii. I did not see another edition after the two articles cited above. The radio was another source of information, commentators Gabriel Heater and Paul Harvey were two radio personalities then.

Finally, we could always get news and information, accurate or not, from the local barbershop and beauty shop. Individuals who could afford subscriptions to *Ebony, Jet and Sepia* were aware and exposed to news and information about the world on a much broader scale; these magazines featured national and in some cases international news about people of color. Consequently, they were sources of pride in the community. Often when new magazines were received, the discarded ones were read by neighbors who could not afford paid subscriptions. In addition to *Ebony, Jet and Sepia* subscriptions, a limited number of individuals who were members of the National Association for the Advancement of Colored People (NAACP), received the official magazine *CRISIS.* Perhaps an even smaller number of individuals purchased *Look, Reader's Digest and Saturday Evening Post.* Parents of classmates or neighbors who worked out of town, namely in Dallas and Houston, would bring old copies of the *Dallas Morning News and the Houston Chronicle* home; thereby providing locals an opportunity to read about events, peoples and places beyond Bryan, Texas.

Chapter 10

City Transit: Transportation

According to the Handbook of Texas Online, in 1910 the population of Bryan reached 4,132; this was a total figure.(Handbook of Texas Online 1910, n.p.) This growth in population caused the city to build an interurban railroad to College Station. The interurban railroad operated until it was replaced by bus service in the 1920's. But the literature review did not reveal an ongoing history of city bus service after the 1920's. (Handbook Of Texas Online 1910, n.p.).

However, during the 1950's there was a bus service, not sure if it was city or private, that operated inconsistently for a period of time. The bus provided transportation to and from the Eastside to Westside and to College Station. It was the principal mode of transportation for citizens without private vehicles; there were many. The designated bus routes were along the three main arteries in the African-American neighborhoods, Pierce, East and West 19th Streets and W. San Jacinto Highway and back downtown to 26th Street; this was the transfer point for inter-city as well as College Station. Limiting bus routes to Pierce, 19th Streets and San Jacinto Highway meant patrons had to walk considerable distances to catch the bus. As an example, patrons living on the far end of Waco Street and Pierce Street extended had a rather long walk to the Pierce Street bus stop. The same was true for customers who lived at the far end of West 15th, 16th and 17th Streets. In addition, walking from home to the bus stop, domestic workers (women mostly) had to walk to the places of work after they got off the bus. This same trek was repeated for individuals after a long work day.

Another limitation to the bus service was its hours of operation; as recalled, it operated from about 7:am to 10:pm Monday – Saturday, and the Saturday hours may have been even shorter. Citizens whose work day began before 7:am were not served by bus transportation. Also, patrons who worked until after 10:pm which was the situation for some café employees (my aunt included), worked late shifts after bus operations ceased for the day. Also, individuals who worked nights at Texas A and M University (Texas A and M College) Memorial Student Center (MSC) Bowling Alley were vulnerable to restricted bus hours of operation. The bus service between Bryan and College Station (as recalled) ceased at 10:p.m., no later than 11:p.m. and earlier in the city. Patrons coming from their jobs at night, again, had to walk from downtown to their individual communities. Such walks in some situations for some were quite a distance. The limited bus routes, schedules and hours of operation were most burdensome and not compatible with customer needs. Nonetheless, while having to walk rather long distances to catch the bus was considered an inconvenience, real health benefits were realized.

Chapter 11

Elected Officials

"Fear the man who feels himself a slave
He'll want to make a slave of you" (Holt 1972, n.p.)

While Brazos County had elected African-American officials, Bryan did not have a sustained line of elected city officials until 1968. According to Paul McKay, Brazos County elected Mr. Dennis B. Ballard to Commissioners Court seven times from 1880-1904. (McKay 1986, p.105) McKay also informs us that another "black" man, Mr. H.M. Maddox joined Ballard on the Commissioners Court in 1888. (McKay 1986, p.105) In addition to Commissioners Ballard and Maddox, an African-American named Mr. Elias Mays represented Brazos County in the Texas House in1879 and 1889.(McKay 1986, p.105) In the 1880's, Mr. Willis Van Hook was a Bryan City Alderman, the title used before 1917. (Blair, Summer 2005, n.p.) But on July 28, 1968 Pat Lester (an Eagle staff writer) wrote: **First Negro To Hold Office** (Eagle 1968, p.2) Mr. Harmon "Son"Bell was elected as a Bryan City Commissioner and served from July 23, 1968 to April 13, 1971 and a second time from August 29, 1972 to April 27, 1976. Bell served as mayor pro tem from April 8, 1969-April 13, 1971. The title City Commission was changed to City Council on April 10, 1973. (Borden 2005. p.28). As Bell was going off the Council for a second time, Mr. Ples Turner joined the Council for a ten year stint; he too served a second time. Other African-Americans who have been elected to the Council are: Mr. Edward L. Aycox, Mr. Paul Madison, Sr. and Mrs. Annette Stephney, the first African-American female (who died in October of 2009) served as Mayor Pro Tem. Paul Madison, Sr. serves on the Council currently, (at the time of this project). Data sources for the 1880's on elected African-American officials, while incomplete, indicate city titles for elected officials in 1880-1917 changed from Alderman to Commission Manager from 1917-1973 and changed again in 1973 to its present title of Council or Councilman. (City of Bryan Ordinance No. 82)

National Association for Advancement of Colored People and Negro Chamber of Commerce

In addition to the Colored Library Association, mentioned in section on Recreational Activities, African-Americans organized the first chapter of the National Association for the Advancement of Colored People (NAACP) in 1919 and Negro Chamber of Commerce in 1928. An article in the April 30, 1919 edition of the Eagle, records the following accounts:

> On Sunday afternoon the Colored people of Bryan and Brazos County met at the New Chapel Baptist Church for the purpose of forming a branch organzation of the National Association for the Advancement of Colored People (NAACP) for Bryan and Brazos County. Reverend S.E. Diggs, acting as master of ceremony, called the meeting to order, after which the purpose of the meeting was explained by I. N. White. The matter was fully discussed by all present and it was definitely decided to organize a branch of the national association. (Eagle, n.p.).

The article explained individuals joining the newly formed organization paid one dollar or more. A second meeting was held on May 5, 1919, at Shiloh Baptist Church.

I. N. White, the first NAACP President, published an article in the Eagle in October 1919 that was written with eloquence and tact. His article was labeled as an adverstiment in that it noted several front-page articles in the fall of 1919 had reported incidents of racial violence in Arkansas and Nebraska, as well as Texas. He was attempting to ease any fear and suspicion of local (blacks) African-Americans and the newly organized NAACP. Portions of his article are as follows:

> October 6, 1919- As to the history of Bryan for the past of years that I have lived here, it has been, for the most part, very, very commendable indeed in

> respect to general conditions affecting relations of the races. Bryan and Brazos County enjoy a record to be envied by every county surrounding, and for that matter, the great commonwealth of Texas must with pride point to the record of this county and boast of the race conduct of this child it's raising, while many of the more prosperous centers, richer by endowment and more attractive by popular bequest, have been writhing in turmoil, blood and great sin to the utter shame and disgrace of the parent mother Texas. "In the meanwhile, we, the citizenry of this county, have looked on with awe-stricken eyes, shuddered with dismay, and have hidden our faces in skies effaced by lawless practices. We take pride in the thought that, should Texas be called upon by civilization to present proof of her better self, Brazos County would be her best offering 'en sample' for inspection, and I dare say it would inevitably be chosen. This does not mean to condone crime and whatever of injustices that may have been measured to members of either race; for Brazos County, like a child of a household, is guilty of mistakes and wrongs and has strayed at times from the teaching of its mother evinced in her constitutional precepts. But she has never permitted her self to wander so far away from the path of rectitude that she failed to hear the pleas of her broken-hearted mother, the constitution, and heed the call to return to sane and equitable methods of procedure.... The Colored people have no secrets to withhold. Their organizations are as wide open for inspections as their churches. In fact, inspection is what they prefer...We ask for more encouragement and less distrust....Our consciences are unfettered and our motives as pure as in the days when the serenity of peace possessed the land. (Eagle, n.p.).

The Chamber of Commerce was another organization formed by African-Americans in Bryan. It was headed by William A. Hammond, Sr., the medical doctor who founded the only hospital for African-Americans in Bryan, Texas. According to a May 6, 1929 article in the Eagle:

> It was largely through the activities of the Negro Chamber of Commerce in Bryan that sufficient funds were made available to secure full time services of the Negro Nurse, Miss. Ethel Butler in Brazos County. The good work she Is doing here is convincing evidence of the need for public health Work among the Negro (Eagle, n.p.).

In the same article were names of the Chamber members headed by William A. Hammond. They included physician colleagues of Hammond, A.E. Thompson and J.M. Franklin; dentists I.A. Carter, P.R. Johnson, Principal E.A. Kemp and R.C. Neal, Assistant Principal of the Bryan Public School for Colored and teachers, Mrs. Fannie Diggs, Mrs. Sadie Thomas, Mrs. Lola Sadberry, Mrs. Juanita Martinez, Mrs. Mary Keatts and Mrs. Ada Hall. In addition, Chamber membership included ministers, J.W. Rhodes, S.E. Diggs, L.A. Greenwood, E.M. Griggs, who was also Superintendent of the Bryan Orphan Home, O. H. Bean, E.C. Ransom, R.L. Sadberry, G. O'Neil and J.E. Smith. Other members included Ethel Butler, county health nurse (mentioned in section on Hospitals and Medical Care), H. K. Harnsberry, county agricultural agent (co-chairman of Library Association), F.D. Benson, F. Osborne, George Wiley, John Lev Thomas (life insurance), Mrs. Josh Green, (fraternal insurance), J.H. Anderson (fraternal insurance and farmer), and A.S. Keatts (real estate and fraternal insurance). Farmers Heslip and John (Sadberry Estate), Earnest Sheets, M.S. Bradley, Joe Tiggs and Charles Hays, grocery merchants Arthur Neal and C.G. McGowan. Paving contractor Fred Martinez, builders and contractors John Jackson, Tom Siler and Walter Brown, shoemaker A.B. Evans and garage operator Marion Payne. Still other Chamber members were café owners William Harrison, Henry Turner, Ernie Johnson, H.Y. Page and hotel owner Tommie Turner and Joe Cooper and Earnest Cass tailors; barbers R.B. Goosby (Pioneer Barber Shop), Henry Crawford, H.C. Mosley and William B. McQueen and Henry Jenkins (mentioned in section of downtown businesses), porter Bremond Triggs and cabinet maker Jethro Hatchett. (Eagle, n.p.)

Chapter 12

Principals, Teachers and Staff

E.A. Kemp Junior-Senior High School built in 1930. Renamed R.C. Neal Junior High after the new senior high school was built in 1961.

From 1885 to 1930 the principals of Bryan Public School for Colored were Mr. A.H. Colwell, Mr. Paul Landry, Mr. Elijah Alonzo Kemp and Mr. Robert C. Neal. From 1931 to 1961 the principals of E.A. Kemp Junior-Senior High School were Robert C. Neal and Mr. Colquitt D. Yancy. From 1931 to 1970 the principals of Washington Elementary School were Mr. Lon Nash, Mr. Edward H. Knox, Sr., Mr. Thomas W. Cole, Sr. and Mr. Oliver Wayne Sadberry, Sr.

Pictures of Mr. A.H Colwell and Mr. Pal (Paul) Landry the first two principals of Bryan Public School for Colored were not available. Nor were pictures of Mr. Lon A. Nash and Mr. Thomas W. Cole, Sr. but pictures of all succeeding principals were and are included on the following pages. Mr. Elijah Alonzo Kemp and Mr. Robert C. Neal served as the third and fourth principals of Bryan Public School for Colored. Mr. R.C. Neal was assistant principal and became principal after the death on Mr. Kemp in 1929. He was also principal of the new E.A. Kemp Junior-Senior High built in 1930 and named in 1931. He was followed by Mr. Colquitt D. Yancy.

When E.A. Kemp Junior-Senior High opened, the former Bryan Public School for Colored was renamed Washington Elementary School in 1931. Principals of the newly named school were Mr. Lon A. Nash, and Mr. Edward H. Knox, Sr. who served from 1934-1943. He was followed by Mr. Thomas W. Cole, Sr. who was principal until Mr. Oliver Wayne Sadberry, Sr. who became principal in 1949 and served until 1970. In 1949 George Washington Carver Elementary School was built on the Westside and the first principal was Mr. Colquitt D. Yancy; he was followed by Mr. Otha Byrd.

E.A. Kemp Senior High School built in 1961.

In 1961 the new E.A. Kemp Senior High School was built on W. 19th; and its first principal was Mr.Colquitt D. Yancy, and Mr. Claude L. Scurry was the assistant principal. Mr. Yancy was followed by Mr. W.D. Dunn and the assistant principal was Mr. James Rose. After the new senior high school was built the former E.A. Kemp Junior-Senior was renamed R.C. Neal Junior High. The principals of Neal Junior High were Mr. Ulysses S. Morgan, Dr. Wendell Davis, Jr. and Mr. Claude L. Scurry, who was the last principal before the schools were desegregated in 1971.

Great care and effort were made to confirm and or recall all the dedicated and devoted principals and teachers who helped educate generations of African-American boys and girls from 1885-1971. However, some names could not be found, but many were part of the Bryan Public School for Colored, E.A. Kemp Junior-Senior and the Senior High Schools. Others were part of Washington and George Washington Carver Elementary Schools. Still others were a part of all the schools for African-Americans, until desegregation in 1971. Together they provided hundreds and hundreds of combined years of service to the community. It was not uncommon to find individuals whose careers in education spanned between 30-45 years in the classroom or a combination of classroom and school administration.

Elementary School Principals

From 1885 to 1930 the principals of Bryan Public School for Colored and from 1931-1970 Washington Elementary Schools, as stated earlier, were: A.H.

Mrs. Louise Anderson

Mrs. Lennis Bailey

Mrs. Olivia Banks

Colwell, Paul Landry, Elijah Alonzo Kemp, Robert C. Neal, Lon A. Nash, Edward H. Knox, Thomas W. Cole, Sr. and Oliver Wayne Sadberry, Sr. Some of the teachers were: Anne Alberson, Pearl Brooks, Mamie Burrows, Beatrice Calhoun, Irma Carter, Corrine Cass, (Mrs.) Dickson, Fannie Diggs(also Fairview School Principal), Ada Ford, Lenora Green, Ada Scott Hall, Juanita Cunningham Hunter, Mary Keatts, Carrie King, Juanita Martinez, Lelia Nash, Willie Lee Nea,l wife of Robert C. Neal, Atoy Peterson, James Phillips, Johnnie L. Pillows, Cornelia Reed, Neal Reed, Lola Sadberry, Annie Stoval, (Mrs.) Tates, Mabel Thomas, Lula Callier, Ella Mae Gregg, Leila Hall, Hattie Jackson, Vernell Jackson (not related), Eloise King, Sylvia McIntosh, Lorraine Ocheltree, Doris Scurry, Jessie Mae Walton, Geraldine Toliver, Clara Smith, Lucille Byrd, (Mrs) Oliphant, Mr. Lawrence King, and E.J. Noble was custodian.

Mr. Otha Byrd
George Washington Carver

Mr. Richard Calhoun

Mrs. Rose Cowan

In 1931 Bryan Public School for Colored was named E.A. Kemp Junior-Senior High School and in 1961 a new E.A. Kemp Senior High was built. From 1931-1960 and from 1961-1971 some of the teachers in alphabetical order were: Myrtel Allen, Louise Anderson, Edward Aycox, Lennie Bailey, Olivia Banks, Fred D. Batts (also principal of Fairview), Margaret Bell, Samuel C. Brisco, Ellen Buttrill, Richard, Calhoun, Minnie Clopton, Rose M. Cowan, Hazel Daily, Robert Guyden, Ruby L. Handcox, Betty J.D.Hatchett, Marion Haynes, Jimmy

Dr. Wendell Davis, Jr.
Second Principal of R. C. Junior High School

Mr. W. D. Dunn
E. A. Kemp Senior High

Mr. Robert Guyden

Herron, Loma Hodges, James Johnson, Troy Johnson, Willa. E. Johnson, Major Jones, Irene Lane, Edessie McClendon, James McClendon, Willie Moore Jr., Hardy Ray Murphy, Willie Lee Neal, A.K. O'Neal, Royce Pace, William Portis, Adolphus R. Price, Mell Pruitt, Freddie Mae Robinson, Claude L. Scurry, Imogene Sharp, Charles A. Shead, Alma H. Simmons, Dolores Stubberfield, Edna Earle Tarrow, Cora H. Tennant, Lloyd. Thomas, Sadie E., Hiawatha Webber, Bernice Webster, Waymon Webster, Robert Wilson, Cecil Wooley, Johnnie L.Wyatt and Dolores Yancy, wife of Colquitt Yancy. Sylvia Sadberry was secretary. Walter Carr, Johnny Damon, and Henry Sims were custodians, and Johnnie M. Jackson and Elizabeth Sterling, lunch-room staff.

Three of the early teachers at Washington Elementary were: Left to right: Mrs. Corine Cass, Mrs. Juanita Martinez and Miss. Mabel Thomas.

In1949 George Washington Carver Elementary School opened and from 1949-1971 the principals were: Colquitt D. Yancy, Otha Byrd and William G. Hall was assistant principal. Some of the teachers were: Anne Orabel Alberson, Estelle Adams, Shirley Birdsong, Inez Daniel, Annie Mae Grays, Inez Grays, Vernell Jackson, Katie Johnson, Mabel Knox, Lila Lane, Teresa Love, Ethel

Mr. William G. Hall
Assistant Principal George Washington Carver

The Bryan Public School for Colored was a frame building, built in 1885 and burned in 1914. It was replaced with a brick building circa 1915.

Mrs. Ruby L. Handcox

Mrs. Bettye J. Hatchett

Mr. James Johnson

Mr. Troy Johnson

Morgan, Willie Lee Neal, Blossie T. Phillips, Doris Scurry, Maggie Sheppard,* Ethel Shipmon, Eudora Smith, Mazie Nell Smith, Anne Sterling, Dolores Stubberfield, George Vaults, Tommie Williams, Dolores Yancy and Ethel Miller, Cafeteria. *Prepared to do doctoral study at Texas A and M University

After E.A. Kemp Senior High School opened in 1961, E.A. Kemp Junior-Senior High became R.C. Neal Junior High School. From 1961-1971 the principals were: Ulysses S. Morgan, Dr.Wendell Davis, Jr. and Mr. Claude L. Scurry as mentioned before. Some of the teachers and staff were:

Pictured are some of the early teachers at Bryan Public School for Colored. From left to right: Mrs. Mary Keatts, Mrs. Juanita Hunter, Mrs. Ada Scott Hall, Mrs. Irma Carter and Mrs. Atoy Peterson.

Pictured is the brick building that replaced the frame building built in 1885–Bryan Public School for Colored. It was renamed Washington Elementary School in 1931 and remained until it burned in 1970 and was not replaced.

Mrs. Anne Alberson-English Mrs. Linnie Bailey-Art Mrs. Ellen Buttrill-Reading Mr. Carey Cauley-History Mrs. Myrtle Crosby-Music Mr. Iney C. Cunningham-Science Mrs. Inez Grays-Special Education Mrs. Laura Jackson-P.E Mr. Vernell Jackson-Coach Mrs. Willa Johnson-H.M. Mrs. Lila Mae Lane-Math Miss. Lollie Marshall-Nurse Mrs. Lorraine Ocheltree-English Mrs. Effie A. Perry-Math Mr. Bobby Joe Perry-Coach Mrs. M. Sanders-Math Mrs. P. Sewell-Reading Mr. C.A. Shead-Band Mr. Lloyd Thomas-Agriculture Mr. Elvin Tyrone-World Geography Mrs. Ora Waldron-English Mr. John Watkins-Math Mrs. E. Wilson-Librarian Mrs. Gloria White, Secretary.

Mrs. Willia Johnson

Mr. E. A. Kemp
Bryan Public School for Colored

Mr. Edward H. Knox, Sr.
Washington Elementary

Mrs. Irene Lane

Mrs. Edessie McClendon

Mr. James McClendon

Mr. Willie Moore, Jr.

Mr. Ulysses S. Morgan
First Principal of R. C. Neal Junior High School

Mr. R. C. Neal
Bryan Public School for colored and E. A. Kemp Jr-Sr High

Mr. A. K. O'Neal

Mrs. Mel Pruitt

Mr. James Rose
E. A. Kemp Senior High Assistant

Mr. O. W. Sadberry
Washington Elementary

Mr. C. L. Scurry
E. A. Kemp Jr-Sr High
Assistant and Principal of
R. C. Neal Jr High School

Mrs. Alma H. Simmons

Mr. Charles A. Snead

Mrs. Delores Stubberfield

Mr. Edna Tarrow

Mrs. Cora H. Tennant

Mrs. Sadie Thomas

Mr. Lloyd Thomas

Mrs. Bernice Webster

Mr. Waymon Webster

Mrs. Johnnie P. Wyatt

Mr. C. D. Yancy
George Washington Carver
E. A. Kemp Jr-Sr High

Chapter 13

Dry Toilets, Street Lights, Lamps and Unpaved Streets

"Salvation is being on the right road,
not having reached a destination.(Martin Luther King, Jr.)

For African-Americans, life in Bryan was filled with separates, such as drinking fountains, seating in theaters, buses and trains. In addition, city services such as, sewers, paved streets, and street lights were not evenly available to African-Americans as whites. For example, Bryan built a sewage disposal plant in 1913 to accommodate the western part of the city. (Brazos County Historical Time Line 1850-2000, n.p.) But it was not until years later (1940's -1950's) before a number of African-American neighborhoods were connected to the city sewer system. As a result, dry toilets "out-houses" dotted the landscape throughout both Eastside and Westside communities. But the city employed two African-American citizens, Roger Harris and Jim Day to clean and disinfect the facilities to prevent (control) harmful bacteria from spreading. Another consequence of not being connected to the sewer system was using tin (galvanized tubs) for personal hygiene (bathing) and (laundry) washing clothes. It was common to see throughout neighborhoods women on scrub boards in tin tubs and large black pots of boiling water doing their laundry on weekends.

According to the Brazos County Historical Time Line street light construction was begun in 1919-1925 in residential areas of W.26th Street to E. 26th Street and near Fanin School in 1921. (Brazos County Historical Time Line 1850-2000, n.p.) However, African-Americans lived on the North-end of the city and street lights were not fully installed in the neighborhood until later. Not having street lights did not deter boys and girls from attending the circus located at Highway 21 and Waco Street. But to be safe they would go to the circus in groups. In the meantime, kerosene lamps were the source of light for student homework and parents' bible reading. Parents and older neighbors who could not see well with lamps would ask young people to thread needles and read the bible for them. Kerosene stoves, although not a very good source, were used to cook with and heat. The other alternative sources for cooking and heating were coal and wood. As some families could not afford to buy coal or wood, Guy Barrow's pasture (with plenty of trees) was an abundant source of wood for many families. C.L. Smith and Pinkey Parnell, et al, would cut wood by the cord and sell to families who could afford to buy.

In the absence of electricity, the option was ice boxes to prevent perishable foods from spoiling and keeping beverages cold. During this time there were two ice delivery men, Guy Barrow and Ira Mickens. One of my tasks was to empty the water pan from melted ice before it was full. On many occasions the family would awaken mornings to find water had overflowed all over the linoleum covered floor. Guy Barrow delivered ice in a horse drawn wagon in 25 and 50 pound blocks; in the Texas heat the ice would melt rather quickly. Ira Mickens delivered ice much faster in a truck; the benefit was ice would last longer after purchased. Mr. Barrow stopped delivering ice soon after Mr. Mickens established a loyal customer base.

Another marked disparity in African-American neighborhoods was unpaved streets. Although downtown Main Street was paved in 1915, when it rained children had to trudge muddy streets to school.(Brazos County Historical Time Line 1850-2000, n.p.) What was worse yet, at night the streets were dark since there were no lights. Students who lived on the Eastside at the far end of Waco Street had a difficult time trying to get to E.A. Kemp Junior-Senior High located on the Westside. The same was true for students who lived on the Westside at the far end of California Street, (before Carver was built) trying to get to Washington Elementary School on the Eastside.

Chapter 14

Ironies-Contradictions-Paradoxes (Signs and Back Doors)

There were two signs (Colored and Whites Only) prominently displayed at water fountains, bus, and train stations and such places as the library, theaters and restaurants. No matter about the signs and back doors, it was an absolute treat every Saturday to buy a chili hotdog served from the back door. I often thought it ironic that during the Korean Conflict African-Americans left Bryan for induction centers riding at the back of the bus.

Three major constitutional amendments 13th, 14th and 15th contained provisions pertaining to citizenship, representation and the right to vote. (Harley 1992, p.165) The 13th Amendment (1865) forbade slavery in any state of the Union. The 14th Amendment (1868) stipulated all persons born in the United States are U.S. citizens and cannot be deprived of life, liberty, property without due process of law nor be denied equal protection of the law. The 15th Amendment (1870) forbade states to deny the right to vote to male citizens on account of race, color, or previous condition of servitude. (Harley 1992, p.165) Yet, in 1866 the Constitution of Texas did not allow Negroes to vote or hold public office. It did allow newly freed men the right to sue, be sued, contract and be contracted with. (Tarleton Law University of Texas, n.p.) Although Negroes were allowed to vote later and served in the State House; at one time a poll tax was required to vote, which meant many citizens did not vote because they could not afford to pay the poll tax.

An article in the Bryan Daily on December 7, 1895 reported 31 white schools and 34 "colored" schools in Brazos County. It was obvious white and black schools were separate, but it was clear they were not equal. On October 23, 1913, the Eagle carried the following report:

Figures compiled by County Superintendent T.W. Parker from reports of the rural teachers of Brazos County for the school year beginning September 1, 1912 and ending August 31, 1913: (Eagle n.p.)

- Number of schools taught-White, 34, colored 37, total 71.
- Number of teachers employed –White 53, colored 37, total 71
- Number of pupils enrolled in school-White 1782, colored 1763, total 3545.
- Number of teachers holding permanent certificates-White 9, colored 4, total 13.
- Number of teachers holding first grade certificates-White 19, colored 3, total 22.
- Number of teachers holding second grade certificates-White 25, colored 30, total 55.
- Number of school desks in use-White 1262, colored 57, total 1319.
- Number of volumes in school libraries-white 1086, colored 10, total 1096.
- Amount paid teachers-White $20,299.90, colored $9,298.93, total $29,598.83.
- Amount paid for repairing building school houses-White $3,834.69, colored, $375.11, total $4,209.80.
- Amount paid for schools desks, school supplies, wood, etc. White $1,546.13, colored $69.10, total $1,614.23.
- Estimated value of school property-White $30,189.00 colored $4,042.00, total $34,232.00
- Average length of school term-White 7.5, Colored 5.75.

Of the twelve items compared, colored teachers with second grade certificates is the only one that comes out ahead of whites. Also, when the number of white (53) and colored (37) teachers are added the total is not 71 but 90.

All the information below was taken from the Introductory Issue of The John M. Moore High School Out-Look, Vol. 1, Bryan, Texas, May, 1946, No. 1. (John M. Moore High School May , 1946 n.p.)

In 1945-46 in a survey of Brazos County Schools conducted by Superintendent Luther Pearson, there were twenty-four common districts operating twenty-four white and Negro schools. Eleven of these schools operated no schools at all, causing the twenty-four schools to be distributed in thirteen districts. Of this number ten are for white and fourteen for colored children. There are:

- 18 white school buildings in the county with 50 classrooms and 18 teachers
- All buildings in white schools meet State requirements
- 20 buildings for colored with 49 classrooms all and 43 teachers
- No auditoriums in colored buildings and only 4 meet State requirements

All the buildings for whites have jacketed wood circulating heaters and lighting and ventilation is adequate. There is also plenty of blackboard space, and each child has a desk; however in the colored schools, excepting two districts, all heaters are box heaters, lighting and ventilation is poor and especially in the two largest schools there are two pupils to each desk.

In 1954 the landmark case, the United States Supreme Court ruled in Brown vs Board of Education in Topeka, Kansas that school segregation and the doctrine of separate but equal was unconstitutional . Nonetheless, Bryan Public Schools did not fully integrate or desegregate until 1971 when Stephen F. Austin and E.A. Kemp Senior High Schools merged into what is now Bryan (Vikings) High School High.

Further ironies, contradictions and paradoxes in the life and times of African Americans in Bryan, Texas are reflected in The Handbook of Texas Online, under the title: **Education For African Americans**.(Handbook Of Texas Online n.p.) The following information from this source (**permission to use**) is used to illustrate the point, not as an excuse, for what happened in both the United States and Texas. The Education of African-American children during the late period of slavery, after 1800, was sporadic and unreliable in Texas and in other Southern states. Formal education was practically nonexistent for African-Americans. Before the Civil War most people (white) believed education of African-Americans would lead to discontent and rebellion. A few did support instruction and often volunteered their services. According to the census of 1850, 58,558 African-Americans, representing 27.5 per cent of the population, lived in Texas. Fewer than 1 per cent, or 397 were free, of which 217 were believed to be literate, 20 were in school; and 58 were illiterate adults. There are no actual statistics available on the 58,151 enslaved African-Americans, but available data indicate that a portion of the slave population had been instructed in the basic rudiments of reading and writing.

In 1865, the United States Congress instituted the Freedmen's Bureau. The bureau's primary function was to supervise and coordinate a vast educational enterprise located in Texas, sixteen other Southern and border states, and the District of Columbia. The bureau supervised schools offering classes from the elementary level through college. These schools provided a formal curriculum of arithmetic, reading, writing, history and geography. In addition, a practical curriculum of civics, politics, home economics and vocational training was provided. Most teachers were supplied by the American Missionary Association, with the majority initially coming from the Northern states. Soon thereafter, a few Southern whites and educated African-Americans were recruited to teach in these schools.

In January 1866, Texas began with ten day and six night schools for black children. There were ten teachers with a total enrollment of 1,041 students (many of whom were adults). Six months later, on July 1, 1866, the Freedmen's Bureau in Texas had ninety schools (including day, night and Sabbath schools), forty-three teachers, and 4,590 students attending. John A. Alvord, the first and only inspector of schools and finances for the bureau, described Texas schools during this period as prosperous. He found that Texas freedmen's schools had needed only minimal assistance from Northern states and attributed this to what he perceived as the minimal impact of the Civil War upon the economic base of Texas. By the end of 1870, there were eighty-eight schools (both day and night) in Texas, eighty-five teachers of whom forty-four were African-American, and 4,478 students. In addition, there were twenty-seven Sabbath schools with twenty-eight teachers (twenty-three were black) and 1,350 students.

The advent of schools staffed by Northern white missionaries was not acceptable to all all the Southern white population. Some persons, alarmed by mandatory acceptance of African-Americans in state politics, were vehemently opposed to the Freedmen's Bureau and exhibited their resentment by burning schools and intimidating the missionary teachers. This attitude was not universal in Texas. The Texas teachers' convention of 1866, for example, passed a resolution urging training for the newly freed African-Americans of Texas. Divergences of opinion and fluctuating attitudes were most distinctly revealed in legislative enactments from 1866 to 1876. The Constitution of 1866 provided that the "income derived from the Public School Fund be employed exclusively for the education of white scholastic inhabitants," and that the "legislature may provide for the levying of a tax for educational purposes." The Reconstruction legislature of 1870, by eliminating segregation, gave Texas a single educational system in which all children shared, but in 1873 and 1875 the state legislature repealed most of the laws of the Reconstruction. period.

In 1871, Texas organized a public school system. The succeeding system, formed under the Constitution of 1876, reestablished the segregation of races but made impartial provision for each. Between 1873 and 1893 at black state conventions, African-Americans from all sections of the state met to express their opinions to delineate their needs, and to shape educational policies. Most significant were the Waco and Brenham conventions and the first meeting at Austin in 1884 of the Colored Teachers Association (see TEACHERS STATE ASSOCIATION OF TEXAS). The state Board of Education conducted its first survey of black schools in 1921. At that time, 6,369 pupils were enrolled. By 1925 there were 150 institutions in Texas offering one or more years of high school work for African-Americans; included in this number were fourteen city high schools, six or more country high schools, and high school departments in every junior and senior college. In the 1920's to 1930's the average length of the school term for black children was only about four days shorter than that for white children. However, Texas spent an average of $3.39 or about a third less for the education of African-American students than for white students. During the same period, black teachers were paid significantly less than white teachers ($91.60 a month, compared with $121.03). In 1940 there were 222,715 black pupils in 116 accredited Texas high schools, twelve of which were rated by the Southern Association of Colleges and Secondary Schools. Approximately half of the 6,439 teachers had degrees.

Teachers at George Washington Carver Elementary School in 1969-70 still almost all African-American.

Students in classroom at Washington Elementary school in 1966-67, eighty some odd years later. Still moving forward from behind.

Picture of an elementary school in 1970 looks like a class in 1885 when the first school for colored was built.

Teachers at George Washington Carver Elementary School built in 1949.

Washington Elementary School faculty in 1968 and all but three faculty are African-American, (83) years since the first school for colored was built.

Teachers at George Washington Carver Elementary School the year before full desegregation.

Mr. Otha Byrd, Principal

Chapter 15

Teachers, Parents and Churches: What I Have Learned

"You must step out of the field before
You can see the mud on your feet"___ Chinese

Growing up there were three strong institutions in the African-American community, schools, parents and the church. They operated in tandem and I still believe they are (were) responsible for what students have achieved. In the introduction one of the stated desires was to have a written document about African-American Life in Bryan ready for the reunion of 2010. Preparing this project helped me to remember events and individuals who provided unforgettable guidance and support at critical stages of life. It helped me to better understand the Chinese saying "You must step out of the field before You can see the mud on your feet." It also allowed me to reflect seriously about why students of the Bryan Public School for Colored, E.A. Kemp Junior-Senior High, E. A. Senior High, Classes of the Decade of the Fifty's, 1948 and 49 come back every two and five years for reunions. Furthermore, it helped me to appreciate why students from the Bryan Public School for Colored, (as many as can) and E.A. Kemp Junior-Senior High students come back every five years for the All Schools Reunion.

Perhaps two of the reasons why students come for reunions are in the purpose section of the By-Laws: 1) to retain the identity of E.A. Kemp High and 2) to promote the highest standards of socialization. What are some other reasons why students come back for reunions? One, because now we realize as individuals and collectively, teachers, parents and churches really helped shape what and who we have become. Two, we come to back to just say thanks for starting us on our way. Three, we come back to honor all three because they, we learned later, were preparing us for a world we could scarcely imagine. The importance of each one of these institutions, schools (teachers), parents and churches is demonstrated at each reunion. The reunion starts with a church service; teachers and parents are recognized during the reunion and the reunion ends with a church service. Although our teachers worked under difficult conditions and in dismal situations they were able to instill hope and lift spirits of students who had so little. Teachers not only taught English, history, math and science but inspiration and endurance that would not allow students to quit. They taught inspiration reflected in the following poem of an unknown author:

> "When things go wrong, as they sometimes will, When the road we are trudging seems up hill, When the funds are low and the debts are high, And we want to smile, but have to sigh, When care is pressing you down a bit, Rest if you must-but don't quit." (Felleman 1979, p113).

They taught us determination, the type of which is demonstrated in the abbreviated lines of Ella Wheeler Wilcox:

> There is no chance, no destiny, no fate can circumvent or hinder or control the firm resolve of a determined sole. (Felleman 1979, p.143).

At E.A. Kemp teachers treated students with respect and dignity, we were not marginalized. It was our preparation ground for learning how to live with others; the golden rule and limits were something self imposed. Kemp High is where students learned they had promises to keep and miles to go before they could sleep. The teachers helped students understand the meaning of words epitomized in "Heights of great men and women were not reached in sudden flight, but they, while others slept, toiled through the night." (Inarguration of James Renick, as Chancellor of North Carolina Agricultural State University in 2000).

It is amazing today that some young people of privilege and wealth experience epidemic rates of depression and anxiety. They lack a sense of authentic self; in other words they possess wealth but not mental health. What a stark contrast between them and African-American boys and girls growing up in Bryan, who were for the most part, very confident and self assured. The question is why? Perhaps it was the special hymns: "Blessed Assurance Jesus Is Mine" or "Jesus Keeps Me Near The Cross" or "Amazing Grace." Or was it the song students sang at weekly school assemblies "I Come To The Garden Alone Where The Dew Is Still On The Roses." Hymns that were heard and sung at school and home that helped to create a vital balance.

Other reasons why individuals come back to reunions are triggered by memories of Sunday Church School and Vacation Bible School experiences at Allen Chapel, Lee Chapel, Peaceful Rest and Shiloh located on the Eastside. The same is true for individuals on the Westside who participated in Sunday Church School and Vacation Bible School at Pleasant Grove, Galilee and New Chapel. After all, the churches, parents and teachers were the foundational blocks upon which character was built and life compasses set. The church experiences and parents taught us to "Lean On the Ever Lasting Arm," "Truth Crushed to Earth Shall Rise Again, Truth Forever on the Scaffold, Wrong forever on the Throne,Yet that Scaffold sways the future, and behind the dim unknown Standeth God within the shadow, Keeping watch above his own." (Lowell, James R. p.21). What parents, especially mothers taught as part of the trilogy is epitomized in the modified words of Langston Hughes' Poem Mother to Son:

> "Life won't be a crystal stair It will have tacks in it And splinters-boards torn up, floors that are bare. But all the time you must keep Climbing on-reaching landings and turning corners. And sometimes going in the dark, where there aint no light."

This project, as do reunions, afforded an opportunity to return to what are often referred to as the "good old days." A chance to travel back in time and space to recall activities, friends and situations that were happy as well as sad. Some of the happy times were attending home-coming parades, football games, socials afterwards, Knox's Place, a first date with a special boy or girl, prom night and graduation. This experience also provided an opportunity for me to safely review the past and the distance traveled since leaving Kemp High. It also reminded me of how far we have yet to go.

Finally, students come back to E.A. Kemp reunions because attendance at Kemp High is another one the commonly shared experiences . No matter where you lived in Bryan, Eastside or Westside or surrounding areas, Kemp for many years, was the only high school for African-Americans until after 1971.

Barbara F. Mosley Cooper Reunion 2000 Church Service

James E. Martin, former E. A. Kemp student relaxing at a reunion picnic in 2000.

Reunion 2006 - Front Center: Isaiah Phillips, Back: L-R: John L. Williams, Rastine Calhoun, James C. Mosley and Oswell Person

Reunion 2007 - Front Row: L-R: Irma Kearney, George Bell, Sarah Graham, Willie Ada Hickman. Second Row: L-R: Willie Alberson, Willie Taylor, Unknown, Marfaret R. Rucker. Third Row: L-R: Faye T. Smith, Louise Dix, Leroy Sterling, Oswell Person and David Taylor.

Chapter 16

Brazos County-
Bryan, Texas Populations

According to some historical evidence African-Americans played a vital part in the initial and continued economic development of Brazos County, but their influence was limited because of segregation. (Brundige 1986, p.11) In 1890 the number of African-Americans reached 8,845 the first and only time in its history that Brazos County experienced a black majority. (Handbook Of Texas Online 1890, n.p.). Based on census information taken from the Handbook of Texas Online From 1900-2000 the total populations of Brazos County and Bryan, Texas continued to grow. But, disaggregated figures for the African-American population were only found in several documents reviewed for this project. However, the 1900-2000 population information below was taken from the Handbook of Texas On Line.

1900-Brazos County Census reports Brazos County Population 18,859
Bryan Census reports Bryan's population 3,589

1910-Brazos County Census reports Brazos County Population 18,919
Bryan Census reports Bryan's Population 4,132

1920-Brazos County Census reports Brazos County Population 21,975
Bryan Census reports Population 6,307

1930-Brazos County Census reports Brazos County Population	21,835*
Bryan Census reports Bryan's Population	7,814
1940-Brazos County Census reports Brazos County Population	26,799
Bryan Census reports Bryan's Population	11,842
1950-Brazos County Census reports Brazos County Population	38,390
Bryan Census reports Bryan's Population	18,102
1960-Brazos County Census reports Brazos County Population	44,895
Bryan Census reports Bryan's Population	27,542
1970-Brazos Census reports Brazos County Population	57,978
Bryan Census reports Bryan's Population	33,719
1980-Brazos County Census reports Brazos County Population	93,588
Bryan Census reports Bryan's Population	44,337
1990-Brazos County Census reports Brazos County Population	121,862
Bryan Census reports Bryan's Population	55,002

*Slight loss in county population, no explication

The racial make up of the 2000 population in Bryan, Texas was 64.65% (65%) white and 17.7% (18%) African-American. (Bryan, Texas Census 2000, n.p.) The U.S. Census of Bryan reports the total population of 69, 036. (U.S.Census 2005, n.p.)

Chapter 17

Surprise Findings

Additional information about events and people discovered while doing research that may be of interest. The dates and events from 1865-1970 were taken from the (Brazos County Historical Time Line) and recorded below. Later information about events, people and places after 1971 was confirmed or verified through interviews and site visits.

1865-December	W.W. Davis opens a Freedmen's school in Bryan.
1867-February	Brazos County: Stephen Curtis, an African-American, elected as delegate to the State Constitution Convention.
1870-September	Shiloh Baptist Church purchase land.
-December	Bryan: Conf. of African-American Methodist Episcopal Church (AME) meets.
1874-March	Bryan:City sells the "Freedmen Burying Ground" to local church.
1875-February	Stearne Chapel African-American Church is given land.
1877-December	Bryan: Conference of AME Church meets.
1878-September	Brazos County: An African-American temperance organization is founded.

1878-November	Brazos County: Elias Mayes, an African-American, is elected to Texas Legislature.*
1879-February	Cornerstone for Allen Chapel is laid.
1879-August	Rev. S.W. Marston from St. Louis, holds institute for "colored ministers."
1880-October	Bryan public school for "colored students has 20 students (not to be confused with Bryan Public School for Colored founded in 1885).*
1882-December	Bryan: Conference of AME Church meets.
1883-September	Bryan blacks sue for right to ride in first class railroad coaches.
1888-November	Brazos County: Several African-Americans hold office; Elias Mayes is again elected to Texas Legislature, H.M. Maddox and D.B. Ballard are elected county commissioners; Powell Harvey is elected constable.* **(Mayes: spelled Mays in some records)**
1890-June	Brazos County: A.H. Colwell is replaced as a census taker by a white man.
1894-August	Bryan: Principal A.H. Colwell nominated Superintendent of Education by Republican Party.
1894-August	Bryan: Grand United Order of Old Fellows, colored, meets in Bryan.
1896-December	AME Church Conference meets at Allen Chapel.
1898-	Bryan: Shiloh Baptist Church purchases land.
1899-	Bryan: Colored Masonic Grand Lodge meets in Bryan.

1899-June	Conference of AME Church meets in Bryan.
1900-	African-American Deputy Sheriff Levi Neal killed in line of duty.
1900-February	Sewage disposal plant completed.
1901	Bryan: P. (Paul) Landry is promoted to principal of Bryan school (1885 Bryan Public School for Colored).
1903-January	"Colored citizens" of Bryan establish a burial organization.
1903-August	An anti-prohibition club for Blacks is organized.
1904-July	Bryan: The Ancient Order of Pilgrims (colored) meet in Bryan.
1905-June	Brazos County: Pleasant Grove Baptist Church has opening services for new building.
1905-October	Bryan: Farmers Improvement Society of Texas (colored) meet in Bryan.
1906-October	Cornerstone laid for new Lee Chapel building.
1912-	Dr. S.W. Hooks (Black) opens a drug store in Bryan.
1908-September	Local African-American farmers organize a farmer's union.
1913-January	Bryan: The "colored" Y.M.C.A. is organized in Bryan.*
1918-	Bryan Blacks formed a Red Cross Auxiliary.
1918-May	Negro Business League formed in Bryan.
1918-October	Negro Council of Defense formed in Bryan.
1919-February	Brazos County: Colored Ministers Association meets at Shiloh Baptist Church.

1919-April	A local NAACP chapter is organized.
1920-March	Brazos County: Corner stone laid for second Allen Chapel building.
1920-July	Colored Woodmen of the World meet in Bryan.
1922-June	Bryan: Grandview Colored Cemetery opens.
1923-November	Brazos County: A "Good Cheer" organization is formed to help needy Blacks.
1929-June	Dr. William A. Hammond, Sr. elected president of Texas African-American Medical Association
1929-June	Professor E.A. Kemp died.
1931-September	E.A. Kemp Junior-Senior High opens.*
1938-January	Brazos County: A Negro Worker's Club is organized.
-February	Brazos County: African-Americans interested in scouting meet.
1942-April	Ground breaking for Negro Catholic Church in Bryan.
1959-	Bryan: Sadie E. Thomas Memorial Park dedicated.

*Cited in text earlier

According to an article entitled, **The Black Experience in Brazos County,** reported in the (Bryan-College Station Eagle February 8, 1986, p.8) two black newspapers, The Republican and Torchlight were formed between 1895 and 1915. The Republican was founded in 1896 by Rev. R.M. Holmes, who had previously published something called The Watchword; The Torchlight was founded in 1912.

Chapter 18

African-Americans Still Rising Small Businesses and Other Ventures

Some, not all, African-Americans who were not mentioned fully but continued to demonstrate self reliance by establishing small businesses, other ventures, employment, and positions in public schools; government, higher education and the private sector (Corporate America) are indicated below.

Johnny Ellis, class of 1954 started the Trucking and Vending Machine, Inc. Ray Mc Dade, M.C. Scott and Walter, Jr. owned Trucking Companies. Paul Madison, class 1965 was owner of Metals and Business Consultants. Elvin Walker class of 1963 opened Presto Car Wash in 1976 and KWIK KAR Car Wash in 1984. He opened car wash number three in 1991. Elvin also became the first African-American Detective Sergeant on the Bryan Police Force. Jesse Marvin Walker established a Bail Bondsman Office in 1987; and is also owner of Walker and Walker Custom Printing. Irma Rooks Kearney experimented with a "Rent-A-Nanny Service in the 1980's. Melvin Hanks and Family Realtors, and Curry Plumbing, Inc were going business concerns. Willie Idlebird owned Bird's Appliance Services, Ples Turner was a Builder and Contractor. Raymond Johnson; Green and Sons owned service stations. Thomas L. Moore owns an Appliance and Repair Service. Bessie Gibbs Mason owned a Christian Book Store. Ann E. King owns an African-American Book and Specialty Store. Amy Bradley Galloway owned a Domestic Cleaning Service.

Public Schools, Government, Higher Education Private Sector, Corporate

Linda Smith Asberry is Principal of Neal Elementary School; Dr. Sid Garner was Principal of Robert Driscoll Middle School in Corpus Christi, and Woodrow was a school principal in Bryan. George Vaults served at every level in Public School Administration including Superintendent of the Calvert ISD. Bobby Joe Perry, while Head Basketball Coach at E.A. Kemp led the team to district championship in 1968-69. He led Bryan High Vikings to four district championships; two bi-district championships; and was named Coach of the Year in 1972-73. Blanche Barrow and Johnny Robertson taught in American Indian Schools on Arizona Reservations. Beverley Sheppard Lawson is Department Chair of Career and Technical Education in the Fort Bend ISD; and Mildred Ray Davis served as Assistant Superintendent of the Grand Prairie ISD. Queen E. Vaults Shaw was Director of Staff Development in the North Forest ISD. Jo Ann Stephney Jordan served as a public school principal in a Northern California ISD. Barbara Jean Rucker Broussard was a Computer Specialist in the Houston ISD. Clovus D. Pruitt taught in Job Corps, in San Antonio, Texas. Beatrice Potts Young was a School Councelor and Principal.

Nat Dove presenting the Bakersfield Blues Preservation Society Plaque to his former music teacher, Dr. Waymon Webster in 2006.

U.S. Postal employees (since the first African-Americans) LaRue Johnson, Ples Turner, Odis Walton, Sr. and Savannah Williams, have been Charles Walton, Maurice Green, Jr., Cecil Davis Crenshaw and Mattie Robinson Carter. Ernest Moore was in Federal Civil Service in San Antonia and taught in the government vocational training school. Peter Calhoun and Joe Willie Toliver are retired Law Enforcement Officers for the cities of Los Angeles and Seattle respectively.

George Vaults class of 1954 was Superintendent of the Calvert ISD. He was voted Region VI Superintendent of the year in 1994 while serving as Superintendent.

Dr. Wendell Davis, Jr. was an Assistant Professor at Prairie View A and M University; Program Director for Division of Accreditation and Technical Assistance at the Texas Education Agency (TEA). He also served in the Department of Special Investigations at TEA; and the U.S. Department of Education. Dr. Halcyon Sadberry Watkins was an Assistant Professor and Assistant Dean at Prairie View A and M University; and an Assistant Professor at Texas Southern University. Dr. J. (Joe) Willard Toliver was an Instructor at Prairie View A and University; and a Professor at the University of Houston. He was a Professor at Florida A & M University; and Associate Dean at Florida A and M University, and Florida State University Schools of Engineering. Leroy Sterling was an Assistant Professor at Alabama

Principal's Message - It is my sincere hope that as you view the pages of this '70 edition of the Tiger, you will become more aware of the increasing need for quality education within the youth of our community. I, like you, take pride in the many notable accomplishments of the Student Body of "Tigerland." I am particularly pleased with the academic advancements and with the consistently increasing desire of our students to adequately equip themselves for making worthwhile contributions to our society in their life after school. I am convinced that Elmore has the potential in student body, physical facilities, teaching staff, and desire to become the best high school in our state. This worthy goal is now in our reach. Our united efforts will make the desire a reality. - - - Sincerely, George Vaults

A & M University, and Jarvis Christian College. Walter Hollins is an Assistant Professor at Houston Community College.

Dr. Adolph Johnson, Jr. served as Academic Dean Cerritos Community College in California. Barbara Williams Dixon an Instructor at Prairie View A and M University, and Gladys Green Smith served as Associate Dean Los Angeles Trade-Technical College. Melvin Eugene Turner served as an Episcopal Priest at St. Phillips Episcopal Church. Dr. Catherine Martin was faculty at Prairie View A and M University, and Tulane University. Dr. Jerry Guyden is a Professor at City College of New York. Frank Perry was a faculty at Florida A and M; Alcorn University, Mississippi, Texas Southern University, Jarvis Christian College, Fayetteville University North Carolina, Stillman College in Alabama, and Livingstone College in North Carolina. He also studied at the prestigious Julliard School of Music in New York. James Sterling was Assistant Professor at Southern University in New Orleans; and highest ranking African-American in the Marketing Division at Dow Chemicals. He was also a scientist in the Federal Food and Drug Administration. Dr. Darlene Sheppard Abrams served as Dean of the College Education at Langston University in Oklahoma. Dr. Weldon Walton served as Distinguished Faculty of Biology; Science Department Chair, and Vice President for Academic Affairs at Paul Quinn College. O.D. Baker was an Instructor at the Houston Theological Seminary. Willie Pruitt and Cecil Webster were faculty at the West Point Military Academy. Dr. Wauline Pierce Gamble taught Elementary School in the Caldwell ISD, and was Professor of Education at Paul Quinn College.

Mr. Bobby Joe Perry, Head Basketball Coach led the Kemp Varsity Tea to the 1968-1969 District 10 AAA North Zone Championship. Mr. Robert Guyden was the Assistant Coach. Some of the team members were: Stearne Scurry, "Penny" Crawford, Charles Druery, Don Thompson, "Chick" Chatham and Larry Koontz. Mr. Perry also led the Bryan High Vikings to four District Championships and two Bi-District Championships. He was named Coach of the Year in 1972-1973.

Dr. Waymon Webster, teacher, and Dr. Oswell Person, former student, engaged in serious conversation 2002 class reunion.

Ethel Gibbs Batten was Vice President of Human Resources for Lucent Technologies in Warren, New Jersey. She was also Vice President of Equal Opportunity Officer and Human Resources Compliance Officer for America, Canada and Latin America. In addition, Ethel was Human Resources Vice President for Global Diversity Operations in over 140 countries. She trained at The Aspen Institute, Cornell University, University of Michigan and Yale University. Juanita Gibbs Johnson served on the Federal Reserve Board and Margaret Gibbs Brooks was an Assistant Vice President for Urban Banking in Dallas. Howard Gibbs is Labor Relations Specialist for the U.S. Postal Service in Oakland, CA.Leroy Gibbs was in management for General Motors in Los Angeles, James O. Gibbs was the Senior Quality Control Supervisor for General Motors in Los Angles. Margaret R. Rucker Finely was a Supervisor with Texaco Oil Company in Houston. John Latson is a Supervisor at the All Seasons Door and Window Company. Leon Davis was Business Manager for Hod Carriers Local 166 in Oakland, California. Jimmy Leon Tillery was in the executive management tier for the telephone company in California.

Public School Teachers and Administrators not mentioned above who have continued the long line of dedicated (25-40) years of service from the 1930's-1971; are arranged below by name and year of graduation from high school.

Class of 1934
Richard Dix Jordan
Blanche Barrow

Class of 1937
Channie Dix Jordan
Berthenia Ellis Wallace

Class of 1939
Zack Grays

Class of 1942
Ruth Neal

Class of 1945
Irene Shields Mitchell
Earnestine Petty

Class of 1946
Ella Mae Neal Donovan

Class of 1947
Ernestine Petty

Class of 1948
Rosie Rice Greer

Class of 1949
Pearlie Prunella Petty
Martha Potts Scott
Lorraine Sterling

Class of 1950
Imogene Petty
Dr.Wauline Pierce Gamble
Johnnie Petty

Class of 1951
Davis Edwards
Ethel Lillian Jones
Estella Woods

Class of 1952
Dorelia Powell
Gladys Sanders

Class of 1953
Martha Miller Allen
Rosa Rouse Dvis
Mazie Nell Smith Mack

Class of 1954
Doris Green Coleman
Doris Dix
Arthur Dunn
Blossie T Phillips
Katha Robertson
George Vaults

Class of 1955
Iona Potts Griggs
Ann E. King
John Jerome Knox
John Williams

Class of 1956
Billy Ray Smith
James T. Knox*

Class of 1957
Louise Dix
Milton Green
David Littleton
Faye Patterson Sabbs

Class of 1958
O.D. Baker
Etta Duren Jones
Vivian Faye Littleton
Raymond Moore
Lonnie Mulkey
Ona McMillan Sims
Janice Thurman

Class of 1959
Andrew Byrd, Jr.
Bobbie Jean Idlebird
Eddie Mae Phillips
Betty Suseberry Hanks

Class of 1960
James H. Alberson
William G. Hall
Betty Suseberry Hanks
Bobby Joe Perry

Class of 1961
Johnnie M. Moten
Hayward Peterson

Class of 1962
Effie Perry
Eddie Mae Phillips

Class of 1963
Ruby J. Butler
Lessie Gilmore
Wanda Peterson Green
Johnny Robertson

Class of 1964
Albert Griffin

Class of 1965
Myrtle Allen

Class of 1966
Pearl Collins Cavitts
Jo Ann Jordan
Beverley Sheppard Lawson
Robert Person
Karen Walton

Class of 1967
Queen E. Vaults Shaw

Class of 1968

Class of 1969
Gwendolyn Davis
Claudette Scurry

Class of 1970
Vivian Vaults Rawls

Class of 1971
Clovus Pruitt
Lorenzo Scurry

*Became a Registered Pharmacist in Illinois later

Chapter 19

Conclusion: Thoughts and Afterthoughts

Having spent the last, nearly two years, thinking; reviewing documents, interviewing; writing, and rewriting, I am left to reflect on several issues. While I have no new information or comments to make beyond those made in the text. I would like to recap certain points.

First, let's look at what the project was intended or set out to do. It is about segregated public education and African-American life in Bryan, Texas from 1885-1971. It is interlaced with historical facts; recollections and reflections about public schools for African-Americans. The project includes a number of topics such as education, elected officials, recreation; housing, and their impact on African-Americans. While all the topics were important, education and school was more dominant; it was the fulcrum for all other segregated experiences. Segregation made every facet of life unequal, and did not legally change in Bryan, Texas until 1971.

I tried to point out how segregation created a social climate that pervaded African-American life, at many different levels. I tried to document and show how African-American education was experienced through inadequate funding; administration; teacher salary; training, and curriculum. But teachers tried to shelter students from the worse damage of segregation, and prepare them to be successful; to move forward from behind They embraced education, and encouraged students to see it as the means to freedom. Of all the other topics, education for African-Americans was (is) the most important. It dominated the thoughts of teachers; parents, and dwarfed barriers in the way of success. I believe it can be said without contradiction, that education was "sine qua non," in the African-American community. Like nothing else, education offered promise, and a chance to fulfill dreams, in the absence of the material prosperity, that was so prevalent among E.A. Kemp students.

Another objective of this project was to prepare a document that would be a reminder of the commonly shared education and school experiences, from 1885-1971. I wanted to highlight the roles Bryan Public School for Colored; E.A. Kemp Junior-Senior High, Washington Elementary; George Washington Carver Elementary; E.A. Kemp Senior High, and R.C. Neal Junior High, played in the lives of hundreds of African-American boys and girls. I wanted to show, in spite of resistant behavior and indifference demonstrated by too many of the majority citizens, boys and girls succeeded. That is not to say that all majority citizens were indifferent; for example, Mr. and Mrs. D.D. Matthews and Mr. and Mrs. Frank Pierce were decent in every way. In writing this book I learned certain members of the Fererri, Varisco and Waldrop families were generous and helpful too. I learned from some of the individuals interviewed that their were numerous majority families who helped in significant and countless ways.

I tried to show how small African-American business owners, as entrepreneurs, helped to create economic independence from local employers and sustain their families. Also, I tried to show how the small business owners helped to create, directly or indirectly, to an attitude of independence, by providing jobs to individuals in the community. But there is little doubt, that obtaining an education helped African-Americans think independently. The section on E.A. Kemp Alumni Academic Achievement is convincing evidence that students indeed moved forward from behind.

I tried to show how limited job opportunities created housing needs that resulted in substandard living conditions. The substandard housing, ultimately, led to the construction of government projects on both sides of the city. I tried to show how others, namely, elected officials made contributions to the community. I tried to point out some of the ironies, contradictions and paradoxes prevalent in the life of African-Americans as a result of segregation in Bryan, Texas. I tried to honor and recognize teachers, and parents, who with so little, helped greatly to bring us thus far along the way.

Finally, I set out to write about life and times in Bryan, Texas based on facts, recollections, and reflections that encapsulated the vicissitudes of African-American life and times in Bryan, Texas beginning with Bryan Public School for Colored. Whatever level of success achieved or whether I succeeded at all must be determined by you, the readers.

References

Anderson, F. G. and Wakefield, E. A. eds. 2001.The History of Medicine In Brazos County. Bryan, Texas.

______. The History of Medicine In Brazos, County. Bryan, Texas.

Banks, Olivia. In Brundige, G. F. ed. 2006. The Sesquicentennial Edition Brazos County History: Rich Past-Bright Future. Bryan, Texas: Family Foundation.

Battle, T. C. and Wallace, D. M. eds. 2006. Legacy: Treasures of Black History ______. Washington, D.C.: National Geographic.

Black Education in Bryan 1975. Brazos County Historical Commission. *www.brazoscountyhistory.org.*

Blair, John.Volunteer State Guard. (Brazos Guard) Summer, 2005).

Borden, Robert. 2005. Historic Brazos County: An Illustrated History. San Antonio, Texas: Historical Publishing, Network.

Boykin, R. D. 1996. Brazos Valley Italians: A Series of Interviews. College Station, Texas: C and R Publications.

Brazos County Historical Time Line From 1875-1899. (October, 1880). *www.brazosgenealogy.org.*

Brazos County Historical Time Line From 1875-1899. (October, 1880). *www.brazosgenealogy.org.*

Brazos County Historical Time Line From 1900-1919. (January, 1913). *www.brazosgenealogy.org.*

Brazos County Historical Time Line From 1865-1970. *www.brazosgenealogy.org*

Brazos County Historical Time Line From 1865-1970. *www.brazosgenealogy.org.*

Brazos County Historical Time Line From 1850-2000. *www.brazosgenealogy.org.*

Brazos County Historical Time Line From 1850-2000. *www.brazosgenealogy.org.*

Brundige, G. F. ed. 1986. The Texas Sesquicentennial Edition Brazos County History: Rich Past-Bright Future. Bryan, Texas: Family Foundation.

______. The Texas Sesquicentennial Edition Brazos County History: Rich Past-Bright Future. Bryan, Texas: Family Foundation.

______. The Texas Sesquicentennial Edition Brazos County History: Rich Past-Bright. Bryan, Texas: Family Foundation.

______. The Texas Sesquicentennial Edition Brazos County History: Rich Past-Bright Future. Bryan, Texas: Family Foundation.

______. The Texas Sesquicentennial Edition Brazos County History: Rich Past-Bright Future. Bryan, Texas: Family Foundation.

Buford, Michael Dwain. Up From Cotton.

______. Up From Cotton.

Bryan-College Station Eagle, February 8, 1986.

Bryan Colored High School and E.A. Kemp High 1885-1985. Bryan, Texas: Bethune Woman's Club.

Bryan Colored High School and E.A. Kemp High 1885-1985. Bryan, Texas: Bethune Woman's Club.

Bryan Daily Eagle, January 18, 1906. In Borden, Robert. 2005. Historic Brazos County: An Illustrated History, (p.29). San Antonia, Texas: Historical Publishing Network.

Bryan Daily Eagle, March 10, 1939. In Borden, Robert. 2005. Historic Brazos County: An Illustrated History, p. 29). San Antonia, Texas: Historical Publishing Network.

Bryan Daily Eagle, March 19, 1939. In Borden, Robert. 2005. Historic Brazos County: An Illustrated History, (p. 29). San Antonia, Texas: Historical Publishing Network.

Bryan Daily Eagle, October 23, 1913. In Borden, Robert. Historic Brazos County: An Illustrated History, (p.38). San Antonia, Texas: Historical Publishing Network.

Bryan Daily Eagle, April 30, 1919. In Brundige, G. F. ed. 1986. The Sesquicentennial Edition Brazos County History: Rich Past-Bright Future, p.105). Bryan, Texas: Family Foundation.

Bryan Daily Eagle, May 6, 1929, (p.4.). In Brundige, G. F. ed. 1986. The Texas Sesquicentennial Edition Brazos County History: Rich Past-Bright Future. Bryan Texas: Family Foundation.

Bryan Daily Eagle, May 6, 1929, p.106). In Brundige, G. F. ed. 1986. The Texas Sesquicentennial Edition Brazos County History: Rich Past-Bright Future. Bryan, Texas: Family Foundation.

Bryan Daily Eagle, 1956. In A History Bryan Parks and Recreation 1868-2004, (p.2). *www.bryantx.gov.*

Bryan Independent School District. 2002. Alumni Directory. New York: Bernard C. Harris Publishing Company, Inc.

Bryan, Texas 1960 Population. Wikipedia The Free Ecncylopedia. *en.wikipedia.org.*

Bryan, Texas 2000. Census Information. *www.localcencus.com.*

City of Bryan, Texas. 1972. Ordinance Number 82, Amendment 1.

Farris, Sandra. (September 30, 2009). Bryan High School History. (n.p.) *fc.bryanisd.org.*

Farris, Sandra. (September 30, 2009). Bryan High School History. (n.p.). *fc.bryanisd.org.*

Farris, Sandra. (September 30, 2009). Bryan High School History. (n.p). *fc.bryanisd.org.*

Farris, Sandra. (2001-2009). History of Bryan ISD.Bryan, Texas: Bryan Independent School District. *www.bryanisd.org.*

Farris, Sandra. (2001-2009). History of Bryan ISD. Bryan, Texas: Bryan Independent School District. *www.bryanisd.org.*

Farris, Sandra. (2001-2009). History of Bryan ISD. Bryan, Texas: Bryan Independent School District. www.bryanisd.org.

Farris, Sandra. (2001-2009). History of Bryan ISD. Bryan. Texas: Bryan Independent School District. *www.bryanisd.org.*

Farris, Sandra. (2001-2009). History of Bryan ISD. Bryan, Texas: Bryan Independent School District. *www.bryanisd.org.*

Felleman, Hazel. 1979. The Best Loved Poems of the American People. New York: Doubleday. (Original work published 1936).

_______. The Best Loved Poems of the American People. New York: Doubleday. (Original work published 1936).

From Then Until Now. 1990. E. A. Kemp High School Classes Of The 50's Reunion Telephone Directory.

Handbook of Texas Online, (np.). *www.tshaonline.org.*

Handbook of Texas Online, (n.p.). *www.tshaonline.org/handbook/index.html.*

Handbook of Texas Online, (n.p.). *www.tshaonline.org.*

Handbook of Texas Online, (n.p.). *www.tshaonline.org.*

Handbook of Texas Online, (n.p.). *www.tshaonline.org.*

Handbook of Texas Online, (n.p.). *www.tshaonline.org/handbook/online/articles/EE/Kde.2print.html.*

Handbook of Texas Online, (n.p.). *www.tshaonline.org/handbook/online/article/BB/* hcb13.html.

Handbook of Texas Online, (n.p.). *www.tshaonline.org.*

Harley, S., Middleton, S and Stokes, C. M. cons. 1992. The African Experience: A History, (p.165). Englecliffs, New Jersey: Globe Book Company.

Harley, S., Middleton, S. and Stokes, C. M. cons. 1992. The African Experience: A History. Englecliffs, New Jersey: Globe Book Company.

A History Bryan Parks and Recreation 1868-2004, (p.2). *www.bryantx.org.*

A History Bryan Parks and Recreation 1868-2004, (p.5). *www.bryantx.gov.*

A History Bryan Parks and Recreation 1868-2004, (p.7). *www.bryantx.gov.*

A History Bryan Parks and Recreation 1868-2004, p.9). *www.bryantx.gov.*

A History Bryan Parks and Recreation 1868-2004, p. 21). *www.bryantx.gov.*

A History Bryan Parks and Recreation 1868-2004, p.22). *www.bryantx.gov.*

Holt, John. 1972. Freedom and Beyond. New York: Dell Publishing Company.

Hughes, Langston. In Derrick Bell. 1992. Faces at the Bottom of the Well. New York: Basic Books.

Introductory Issue The John M. Moore High School Out-Look. (1946, May, Vol.1, No. 1). Bryan, Texas.

King, Martin L., Jr. In Hooks, Bell. 2001. Salvation: Black People and Love, (p.xi). New York: Harper Collins Publishers, Inc.

Lester, P. In Bryan Daily Eagle July 28, 1968, (p.2).

Lowell, James Russell. In Washington, J. M. ed. 1992. I Have a Dream: Writings and Speeches That Changed the World, (p.27). Glenview, Illinois: Scott Foresman.

McKay, P. Black History. In Brundige, G. F. ed. 1986.The Texas Sesquicentennial Edition Brazos County History: Rich Past-Bright Future. Bryan, Texas: Family Foundation.

________. p. 105.

The Men and Women In WW-II From Brazos County and Aggie Veterans, (n.d.).

Renick, James. Inauguration as Chancellor of North Carolina Agricultural and Technical State University.

St. Joseph's History Bryan Hospital, (n.p.). Bryan, Texas. *www.st.joseph.org.*

Texas A and M University. Spring 2001. In Fulfillment of a Dream: African-Americans At Texas A and M University.

Texas Constitution 1866, Article 8. *tarlton.law.utexas.edu.*

U.S. Census 2005 Bryan, Texas. *www.census.gov.*

Williams, T. H., Current, R. N. and Freidel, A. (1966). A History of the United States To 1877, (p.715). New York: Alfred A. Knorf.

Bibliography

The Chicago Manual of Style. 15th ed. Chicago: The University of Chicago Press, 2003.

The City of Bryan, Texas, (n.d.). History of Bryan, Texas. *www.bryantx.gov.*

Dorsey, Mary. Those Were The Days: Bryan, Brazos County, Texas 1821-1921, 1976.

Felder, Cain Hope. ed. Stony The Road We Trod: African Biblical Interpretation. Minneapolis: Fortress Press, 1991.

Foster, Betty Clements. Bryan Legends and Legacies. Bryan: City of Bryan, 1996.

Foster, Michele. Black Teachers On Teaching. New York: The New Press, 1997.

Gates, Henry Louis, Jr. Colored People: A Memoir. New York: Vintage Books, 1994.

Hayre, Ruth Wright. Tell Them We Are Still Rising: A Memoir of Faith In Education. New York: Wiley and Sons, Inc, 1997.

Hooks, Bell. Bone Black: Memories of Girlhood. New York: Henry Holt and Company, 1996.

Kirszer, Laurie G. and Stephen R. Mandell. Literature. 3rd ed. New York: Harcourt Brace College Publishers, 1997.

Marshall, Elmer Grady. "The History of Brazos County, Texas."Master's Thesis, University of Texas, August, 1937.

Nance, Joseph M. The Early History of Bryan and Surrounding Area, 1962.

Nash, Sunny. Big Mama Didn't Shop at Woolworth's. College Station, Texas: Texas A and M University Press, 1996.

Ogletree, Charles J. All Deliberate Speed: Reflections On The First Half Century of Brown v. Board of Education. New York: W.W. Norton and Company, 2004.

Page, Bill. African Americans In Brazos County 1840-1865. *www.brazosgenealogy.org.*

Palmer, Parker J. The Courage to Teach: Exploring the Inner Landscape of a Teachers's Life. San Francisco: Jossey-Bass Publishers, 1998.

Jackson, A.W. A Sure Foundation: A Sketch of Negro Life in Texas, 1st ed. Houston, Texas.

Person, Oswell and Kritsonis, William Allan. A Brief Analysis of the Historical Development of Higher Education for African Americans. Houston: National Forum Press, 2006.

Randall, J.G. and Donald, David. The Civil War And Reconstruction, 2nd ed. Boston: D.C. Heath and Company, 1961.

Sowell, Thomas. Race and Culture: A World View. New York: Basic Books HarperCollins Publisher, 1994.

Swisher, Carl Brent. American Constitutional Development, 2n ed. Cambridge, Massachusetts: The Riverside Press, 1954.

Watkins, William H. The White Architects of Black Education: Ideology and Power in America, 1865-1954. New York: Teachers College Press, Columbia University, 2001.

Wesley, Charles H. Neglected History: Essays in Negro-American History By a College President. Washington, D.C.: Association for the Study of Negro Life and History, 1969.

Wilcox, Lois Ayne. "The Early History of Bryan, Texas." Master's Thesis, University of Texas, 1952.

Index

Appendix A

Dear Reader:

It was stated in the foreword that I owe an apology to many individuals whose names and contributions are not recognized in this project. This omission does not imply contributions of certain individuals and events were not important. It simply means, at this time I could not find or did not have the information. If in reading this document, you determine that significant dates, events and contributions of alumni are missing and should have been included, please let me know. An Information Respondent Form has been provided for you to supply dates, events; names of individuals and their contributions. Your information will be included in a new chapter.

Once you have completed the form, please mail or e-mail it to me at:

Oswell Person
5901 Riverbend Parkway
Fort Worth, Texas 76112
operson5901@yahoo.com

Thank you very much.

Cordially,

Oswell Person

Appendix B

INFORMATION RESPONDENT FORM

Please provide the information appropriate for each item:

Name: ____

Date of High School Graduation: ____________________

Check Highest Degree Earned:

_____BA/BS

_____Masters

_____Doctorate

_____Ed. Specialist

Check Profession:

_____Teacher _____Lawyer

_____MD _____Priest

_____Dentist _____Pharmacist

_____ Other____________________

Check: Type of Business Owned:

_____Barber Shop ____Cafe ____Service Station _____Appliances

_____Beauty Shop ____Car Wash ____ Grocery Store _____Plumbing Co

_____Printing ____Garage ____Trucking Co _____ Book Store

Check Type of Employment:

_____College Faculty ____CEO _____College Dean ____Pilot

_____Vice President ____Other(Name)___________________________

_____President

List Important Dates, Events and Why?

________________________________ ________________________________

________________________________ ________________________________

________________________________ ________________________________

________________________________ ________________________________

List Names of Teachers And The School Where They Taught:

Bryan Public School for Colored 1885-1930

________________________________ ________________________________

________________________________ ________________________________

E.A. Kemp Junior-Senior High 1931-1961

________________________________ ________________________________

________________________________ ________________________________

E. A Kemp Senior High 1961-1971

________________________________ ________________________________

________________________________ ________________________________

R. C. Neal Junior High 1961-1971

_______________ _______________

_______________ _______________

Washington Elementary School 1931-1971

_______________ _______________

_______________ _______________

George Washington Carver Elementary School 1949-1971

_______________ _______________

_______________ _______________

Your Outstanding Accomplishments:

_______________ _______________

_______________ _______________

_______________ _______________

List Phone Number: _______________

List e-mail address: _______________

Thanks